Pete - some light reading for the holidays!
This is quite a journey for us, and
I'm so honored to be on it with
you (and building upon your 25 years
here). Onward!

Sean.

PRAISE FOR *THE IPO PLAYBOOK*

"Steve Cakebread knows the capital markets like few others, having shepherded three tech companies from private ownership to their IPOs and beyond. Readers seeking to learn strategies and key moves around going public—and what follows—will find valuable information in Steve's insights."

—Stacey Cunningham, president, New York Stock Exchange

"The public market is a public reckoning for businesses, bringing much-needed transparency, governance, and accountability. Steve Cakebread's *The IPO Playbook* is the ultimate guide to taking a company public."

—Marc Benioff, chairman and co-CEO, Salesforce

"It's hard to imagine anyone with more experience going public than Steve. His advice for the entire process—from choosing bankers, to directing a very productive roadshow, to pricing and selecting investors—was perfect. Steve helped me and the entire Bill.com team have an amazing experience. Ultimately, following his advice is the best advice I can give anyone."

—René Lacerte, CEO, Bill.com

"*The IPO Playbook* is essential reading for anyone contemplating a public offering. Pulling from the expertise he gained from leading three successful IPOs, Steve Cakebread lays out how to build teams and set policies, procedures, and controls that support not just a successful public offering but the company's continued growth."

—Kevin Thompson, president and CEO, SolarWinds

"Steve Cakebread's *The IPO Playbook* is a real game-changer for corporate executives interested in creating credibility in the market through an IPO. Steve has transformed disruptive technology business models into monetization opportunities—first with the IPO at Salesforce, then at Pandora, and now as the CFO of a hot startup, Yext. In *The IPO Playbook*, Steve shares practical examples of the IPO process from start to finish and, at the same time, demonstrates the significant advantages not just in securing capital to fund growth but also in attracting key talent who will help lead that growth."

—Michael J.T. Steep, founder and executive director of
the Disruptive Technologies and Digital Cities Program
at Stanford University, author of *First Light of Day*

"Going public is a major endeavor for any company, and Steve Cakebread's *The IPO Playbook* provides a valuable perspective on what it takes to do it right. Steve knows first-hand the many challenges and rewards of going through this process and details step-by-step what is involved in setting a company on the path that creates value for all stakeholders—shareholders, customers, employees, partners, and the community."

—Mark Hawkins, president and CFO, Salesforce

"I know first-hand the value of Steve Cakebread's advice. In *The IPO Playbook*, Steve shares the kind of advice that only someone who has led three successful IPOs could give. He breaks down the considerations on whether or not to go public, the steps to get there, and what to do after the IPO—and presents it in an enjoyable, easy-to-read book. If you want to understand how to do an IPO right, read this book."

—John Rettig, CFO, Bill.com

"Steve Cakebread's book is a unique look behind the magic IPO curtain. As the CFO who took Salesforce, Pandora, and Yext public—companies that made history because of their disruptive technology—Steve was the architect and conductor of complex IPO processes. I've had the pleasure of working with Steve for fifteen years and have seen him in action. This book distills valuable business insight on the inside perspective for the timing and the transition from a private to a public company."

—Dominic Paschel, senior vice president, Yext

THE **IPO**
PLAYBOOK

THE **IPO** PLAYBOOK

An Insider's Perspective on Taking Your
Company Public and How to Do It Right

STEVE CAKEBREAD

SILICON
VALLEY
PRESS

Published by Silicon Valley Press, Saratoga CA
Siliconvalleypress.net

Cover design: Anna Curtis
Cover image: © Shutterstock/Matej Kastelic

ISBN (hardcover): 978-1-7339591-2-4
ISBN (ebook): 978-1-7339591-3-1
LCCN: 2019920409

CONTENTS

AUTHOR'S NOTE

May 29, 2020

Today as I forward this book to my publisher for printing, we are in the middle of a pandemic that has reached every country on the globe and taken the lives of nearly one hundred thousand in the United States alone. The impact of this pandemic will be felt for years to come.

As we slowly recover and rebuild our lives, the stock market will play a vital role in the economic recovery of public and private organizations, retirement funds, and the portfolios of small, individual investors.

Initial public offerings feed the market and create new opportunities for these investors. These public offerings fuel the ingenuity of innovative start-ups that need capital for research and expansion. Also, the public markets provide a wide range of access to capital from additional primary offerings to convertible debt to conventional debt. Being public affords numerous ways to raise capital in challenging times as well as times of growth.

This book is written for the leaders of these promising companies and outlines the process of preparing a successful public offering. It is my hope that these companies go public early enough, so the offering price is affordable not just for institutional investors but also for individual investors.

Stay healthy.

Steve Cakebread

FOREWORD

It has been thirteen years since Yext was founded. Then, we were just a small group of employees, most of us with ponytails, housed in a room on the Upper West Side in Manhattan.

Today, we are an enterprise valued at nearly $2.3 billion, headquartered in a nine-story building downtown in Chelsea, with more than a thousand employees working in offices from Shanghai to Berlin.

Most of all, we are now a public corporation.

Two years ago, we had our initial public offering (IPO). Looking back, it has proven to be a total game changer—both for the access to capital it provided and because it changed the perception of the company around the world. I'm not talking about capital markets here; I'm talking about the markets in which we sell software.

Needless to say, when your company grows that fast, its story is filled with important events and turning points that were crucial to its success. But looking back, going public was the most important turning point in making Yext what it is today.

Unless they have been an intimate part of an IPO, most people see going public only as a liquidation event, where investors, employees, and other shareholders who have labored for years to make the company a success get a big payout for their sacrifices.

That's certainly what I thought in the early days of Yext. Indeed, I never imagined the company going public. It seemed an outdated strategy that had been discredited at the beginning of the century when the

dot-com bubble burst. I didn't even know any companies our age that
had gone public. Most were just working toward a future acquisition
by a big firm.

Looking back, I couldn't have been more wrong. Going public
involves so much more: it makes a company better. The person who
taught me that truth is the author of this book. Steve Cakebread has
a gold-plated reputation as the master of taking technology companies public, beginning with his extraordinary success in doing so at
Salesforce and, of course, Yext.

Steve currently is the most in-demand expert on the IPO process
in the tech industry. In writing this book, he is sharing the insights and
expertise that the hottest start-ups in tech want, the same wisdom he
shared with me while taking Yext public.

Steve taught me dozens of lessons as he put in place the systems
and operations that prepared us for IPO day. Let me share three of
them, all of which Steve explains in depth in these pages.

First, in going public your company gains a lot more credibility.
You establish yourself as a *real* enterprise: stable, reliable, and enduring. When Global 2000 companies look at your financial reports, they
see you're not some fly-by-night start-up. You aren't going to sign a big
bank in, say, Germany without that level of credibility behind you. As
a private company, Yext could barely get an audience with such mighty
institutions, and we didn't understand why. After we went public, suddenly those doors were open to us.

The second unexpected impact was on recruiting. In the two years
since our IPO, we have been able to attract amazing talent, including the president and North American sales director from one of the
world's largest tech companies. This talent is fundamentally different from what we could get when we were a private company, in part
because we now have the capital to put together the compensation
packages that attract top talent.

Finally, maybe the most important impact of going public is that
the process of preparing for our IPO forced us to adopt a greater discipline and to put into place systems that made our company more
efficient and better prepared for the future. I often read comments by
outsiders suggesting the ramp-up to going public is onerous and distracting from the company's core business. I couldn't disagree more:

those systems and practices made us—and continue to make us—a better company.

Certainly, going public is a demanding process. Yes, you need to make major adjustments to comply with new regulations, and you need to deal with analysts and shareholders. But this is hardly unique to going public: in building a great company, you need to make numerous adjustments along the way. Long before we went public, Yext was a different company from one year to the next as we dealt with market changes, new competitors, and changing technologies.

Some of the biggest changes, however, have been in me. I used to spend hours picking just the right color scheme for the Yext web page. Now, I scarcely know how to open my computer anymore. I've instituted a five-minute rule on meetings to maximize the number of decisions I can make each day.

In other words, as CEO, I need to run the company at scale, and the ramp-up to the IPO trained me to do that.

I suspect that many start-up executives fear that by going public their companies will lose the vitality and spontaneity that characterize entrepreneurship. They are not entirely wrong: there is a need for greater predictability and detailed reporting to assuage investors and deal with regulatory demands. But if entrepreneurs are going to continue to grow their companies, they will need the professionalism and predictability that being a public company requires.

Trust me, the passion and energy are still there, in many ways more so. As Steve describes in these pages, there is an enormous emotional reward in building something powerful, successful, and enduring rather than merely making a few bucks by selling your creation off to some other company into which it will disappear forever.

I should also add—and it is implicit in Steve's narrative—that going public gives you an added perspective that staying private never will. For example, before you go public, you go on the road show, and you meet with *everybody*. The road show is crazy: it's a two- to three-week marathon. You hold ten meetings a day, plus lunches and dinners. You're continuously pitching the company until you can't talk anymore, and then you do it again the next day. Along the way, you suddenly realize that the only difference between an IPO road show and your prior rounds of venture funding is that now some of the people you are meeting are potential *enemies*.

Before, if the venture capitalist doesn't like you, he or she doesn't invest in your company. Fine. You move on.

But now, in the public markets, people are looking not just to bet on you, but perhaps to bet against you. So you have to realize, "Gosh, are they looking to believe in us and buy our stock, or are they looking not to believe in us and drive the price down?" I found that to be a shocking and, ultimately, illuminating revelation. It has guided my business dealings ever since. Not everyone out there is a potential ally, no matter what I believed as an entrepreneur.

The other thing I've learned is that investors are often better at numbers than you are. They can teach you many important things about your business. For example, I'm a product-focused founder; numbers aren't my greatest strength. By comparison, some investors can see things in your numbers that you never even noticed—emerging problems that need immediate attention and budding opportunities you haven't yet spotted.

What Steve taught me is that the IPO isn't the end point but only the beginning. Going public is a big goal, but it is only the first of your company's big goals. I really didn't understand that at the time; I certainly do now.

J. P. Morgan said, "Go as far as you can see; when you get there, you'll be able to see farther." Today we're running toward our current big goal, and once we get there, we'll figure out the next one.

This all began with the Yext IPO. Steve Cakebread led us there. We listened to his words of wisdom. You owe it to yourself to do the same.

Howard Lerman
Yext CEO

THE ROLE OF AN IPO IN A COMPANY'S STORY

Why a book about going public?

After all, despite a recent bump, aren't initial public offerings (IPOs) mostly passé—and a momentary fad? After an explosion of IPOs in the late 1990s, the number has tapered off. Even with a bump in 2018–2019, begun by Lyft and Uber, IPOs remain so rare that even the smallest ones draw headlines, as if they are sightings of a remarkable animal long thought extinct.

Yet, in the pages that follow, I'm going to make the argument that an IPO is the best long-term strategy for most companies, that IPOs are as valuable, and as important, as ever. Perhaps even more so.

That's a bold claim. After all, if an IPO is so useful, why don't very many successful companies—run by armies of smart business and financial people—take advantage of the process? Why, over the last twenty years, through booms and busts and everything in between, hasn't there been a return to the high volume of IPOs that we saw in the 1990s? Why do endless hot, new start-ups choose to pursue acquisition by giant companies, thus being extinguished as independent entities? Why not grow as public companies and perhaps become giants themselves?

As I helped lead my own companies—including Salesforce—through the IPO process, I came to realize that there was a simple explanation: the notion that IPOs are overly expensive, inefficient at capturing capital investment, and filled with risk. This is a *myth.*

If there is one thing I've learned from thirty years of dealing with entrepreneurs, CEOs, and venture capitalists, it is that many rational decision-makers will adopt the common practice of their peers in order to save time and effort, rather than actually investigating what is, in fact, the objective truth. The truth is that selling your company is for many reasons—financial, strategic, and personal—a mistake.

In the 1990s, the opposite attitude was true: companies went to enormous effort—"poison pill" stock strategies, scorched-earth anti-acquisition policies, and other defensive tactics—to keep from being acquired. The consensus was that acquisition was the kiss of death, that whatever money the founders earned on the sale would be a fraction of what they'd make if they stayed independent and built their company into a publicly owned powerhouse. Moreover, it was believed, and it is still true today, that if you were acquired, the acquiring giant would inevitably kill the young company through ignorance and ham-fisted policies.

All of that changed with the dot-com bubble and bust at the end of the twentieth century. As hundreds of newly public corporations imploded and billions of dollars of new wealth evaporated, suddenly the IPO, as the preferred tool for company expansion and validation, became perceived as a dangerous, high-risk strategy. By 2007, as a joke of the time went, every start-up company business plan in Silicon Valley had the same last line: ". . . and then we sell to Google." It was funny, because it was so true.

That's when the current myth became widely accepted: IPOs are too risky. What if the stock price collapses? Why take on the burden of all of those new stakeholders and shareholders with their endless complaints and potential class action suits? Who wants to deal with quarterly reporting, Sarbanes-Oxley (SOX), quarterly analyst calls, and—if you make the slightest mistake—the Securities and Exchange Commission (SEC)?

Frankly, there was just enough truth in that argument—combined with a wary stock market after the dot-com bust—to collapse the number of IPOs in the early years of the century. In an exceptionally volatile equities environment, the perceived risk was just too much. Better to just sell out, take the money—*now*—and run, even if it was a fraction of the return from staying independent.

Such a defensive attitude might have been understandable in the years following the bust. But the number of IPOs remains depressed all these years later, at a considerable cost to entrepreneurs, to consumers, and to society itself.

We now know what an economy looks like when new companies choose to sell out rather than build themselves into powerful, enduring enterprises. Employees of the sold companies are rewarded, but not as they would have been if the companies they founded went public. Fewer jobs are created in the overall economy. Competition is diminished as a small number of giant companies gobble up available startups, making their hegemony ever more complete. Innovation suffers. The economy stagnates as older companies aren't replaced by dynamic new ones.

Not to mention the psychological effect—one that few players consider when they contemplate selling out. All entrepreneurs want to create something great and enduring. So what happens when you turn that dream over to someone else and stand on the sidelines and watch other people take over your life's work? Will that roll of money in your pocket soothe the ache?

THE IPO ADVANTAGE

So why challenge a current business culture that assumes an IPO is the wrong course to take? Why swim against the tide? Here are six big reasons, and I'll bet there is at least one of them you've never considered before:

1. Build a Company That's Recognized

Don't diminish this factor. There is a distinct difference between creating a company that is sold and disappears and building a company that endures and thrives. A big bank account is fine, but being able to point to an established institution and to say, "I built that" is immensely satisfying. Moreover, it helps to define you to your peers and becomes an important touchstone in your legacy.

This is also the case for your employees: pride of ownership runs deep in start-ups. The pride of those founders who were there in an apartment or garage and those early employees who may have joined soon after, and were part of the early years of creation, can be life changing. Creation—not only of the product and services, but of the image of the company, the company values, and the business processes—is one of the most rewarding experiences in business life.

Even now, when I return to Salesforce, I see vestiges of the business processes and organization that I helped to create and many people who helped me build the finance organization. We reminisce about those days as some of the happiest in our careers. The personal connection still remains, even if sometimes the newcomers to a $17 billion company do not know who you are. We know that if not for those who joined the company early, these newcomers would be working someplace else, and possibly with less success. If you are a founder or part of the founding team, the stories, the memories, and the pride are a huge part of your personal success.

2. Share Success

Going public is the best way to reward all of your loyal stakeholders: investors, employees, and even your community. Sharing the success of a growing company is part of the journey. The really great founders know that others contributed to the team and helped the business flourish over time. They also recognize that different people are great at different stages of growth—so the sharing has to both expand as the company grows and reward those who move on.

Interestingly, original founding employees and pre-IPO employees often go on to start their own companies, thus extending the journey of invention and creation to other new companies. In this way, sharing is more than wealth creation; it is a training ground for the next generation of entrepreneurs. The heritage of every start-up is rooted in start-ups from a previous generation.

While this sharing is great for investors and employees and plays a crucial role in growing future start-ups, it also is key to expanding both wealth and employment in society. Has the reduction in publicly listed companies and start-ups over the last fifteen years contributed to our increasing gap between the haves and have-nots? It's a question worth considering. These days, the middle class has fewer opportunities to invest in start-ups (even post-IPO) and participate in their growth and wealth creation. That start-up listing with $100 million in market value creates a significant investment opportunity for a wide range of individuals at lower stock prices, offering the opportunity for unmatched stock appreciation and added job creation as the company grows. At Salesforce, I started when the company had sixty-five employees, and I left nine years later when it had nearly four thousand. At Yext, I started with about a hundred employees, and within two years we had ten times that many, with significant future growth in employment ahead of us.

Instead, today when a "unicorn" company with a market value greater than $1 billion enters the market, with its growth curve slowing and mostly owned by large institutional shareholders, it denies the smaller retail investor and the middle-class access to more reasonable wealth creation. That new wealth is taken by venture capital and private equity—they alone get in early on the high-growth phase of a company. Thus, the highest returns are shared only by a small group of elite investors.

3. Become Known Globally

How do you get a Siemens in Germany to see you as a viable supplier or customer? Internationally, as a private company you remain largely unknown—and unproven. Being listed on the NYSE or NASDAQ legitimizes you in the eyes of the world. You are now perceived as a safe buy, a viable enterprise, with real staying power.

In fact, an IPO often proves to be one of your best lead generators. This comes about because of the extensive coverage for your IPO. On your IPO day, the financial press, both online and traditional media, can disseminate your story to large audiences. That, combined with an exciting web page that investors will encounter when searching for more information on your company, will get the message out about the company.

Properly done, these efforts can attract a large number of sales leads. Further, becoming listed on an exchange implies some degree of stability and viability, which also aids future sales. A company identity bolstered by the legal requirement of the regular reporting of financial information gives a prospective buyer confidence when buying into a new technology or solution.

4. Founder Appreciation

Start a great company and sell it to someone else, and your efforts and achievement will soon be forgotten, buried in the parent company's history, and reduced to a minor line item on your resume. But don't your accomplishments deserve to be recognized and celebrated?

Further, founder recognition affords more opportunities to invent and contribute, not only in other areas of technology but also in the social sector. Take Marc Benioff at Salesforce. Clearly, he founded the first and most successful business-to-business software company in the cloud. But, just as important, because of that success he was able to have a significant impact on the cities of San Francisco and Oakland by funding and supporting children's hospitals in these areas, as well numerous other community services.

Founder recognition also brings the chance to become a founder once again. Elon Musk, part of the founding team at the widely successful PayPal, has gone on to other technology start-ups such as Tesla and SpaceX. He and others have been able to obtain considerable funding for their newest projects because of this founder recognition.

By comparison, when a founder sells out to a bigger company, the founder inevitably leaves the acquiring company. A small press release announces that departure, but little else. What that press release usually leaves unsaid is that the founder left because his or her vision for the company was misaligned with that of the new parent. In other words, the founder is recognized only as another disgruntled employee who has decided to leave—not exactly a positive legacy.

5. Discipline for the Future

Companies that go through the IPO process—an experience that may take a year or more—are often surprised that the very act of putting auditing systems in place, developing the messaging and documentation in the prospectus, streamlining the organization, and answering questions from potential investors on the road show is an extremely useful disciplining process.

Young companies, in their rush to get products to market and capture market share, often get distorted in their operations, stick with inadequate or obsolete monitoring systems, and fail to add the new employees they need for the next stage of growth. The ramp-up to an IPO forces you to revisit all company operations and replace or rebuild those that are past their usefulness. The earlier a company commits to the serious governance required to be a public company, the better.

Often VCs convince founders that it is easier to keep the company private and then sell to someone else rather than deal with the costs of going public. And, in truth, the issues around SOX or public company audits and communications with investors do cost additional money and do take time to get in order. That said, this work for a $100 million company, if done properly, likely amounts to about $4 million a year.

Ask yourself: Are you willing to spend $4 million per year to become a successful public company, rather than make some quick money at the cost of your own reputation, the loss of your employees' success, and the loss of other folks benefitting from your vision of the future?

Growing a successful public company requires systems, administration, fair compensation for your workforce, and a return on investment to all investors (both pre- and post-public). In other words, it is the most salutary process imaginable for creating a great company. A cynic might conclude that, in the world of VCs and private equity, the avoidance of going public is the equivalent of selling the Brooklyn Bridge: it is all about the money and nothing else. If they find a bigger "fool" to buy the company, why bother doing all the hard work to go public?

But if not going public is the agenda, one must ask: Why bother building a business at all? Why not just build a prototype and sell or license the rights for as much money as you can get?

Once, in search of a new opportunity, I visited the founder and his small team at a small, new telecommunications company. We spent the day discussing the company's vision, the market opportunity, and its potential to become a very large, important player in the telecom industry. At the end of our meeting, they took me to see their prototype product. Unfortunately, it had just malfunctioned . . . and burned up. Surely, I told myself, this won't be the only day of interviewing. I'll return in a few days and see the working prototype.

A week later, not having heard from them, I reached out to the company, only to be told by the telephone operator that the company had been sold to a very large and rapidly growing networking company in San Jose for $10 billion. Wow. Needless to say, it wasn't long before the grand vision of the founder and the potential for the young company and its technology to change the game were buried by the acquirer. Meanwhile, most of those billions were collected by the VCs who had backed the company. Such a loss for the employee group who worked so hard to produce the next-generation telecommunications company, and for the potential retail investors who could have participated in the wealth creation of the IPO.

6. Rationalize Valuation

Private companies never really know their actual worth in the marketplace. This is especially true for hot, fast-growing companies where rumor, media hype, overenthusiastic fans, and other promoters often produce a perceived valuation that is way out of sync with reality. This can lead investors to pay too much for their investments—a recipe for class action suits if and when the company momentarily stumbles. An IPO, being the subject of considerable outside analysis and carefully prepared financial tables, sets a real value on the company and stabilizes that valuation over time.

As I've said, going public affords numerous parties the opportunity to participate in the appreciation of value over time—not just the founders and start-up employees, but other outside investors, and the community-at-large. While there are days when the stock market overreacts short-term to a company's successes or shortcomings, over time it properly values the hard work and results of the founder and his or her team of employees.

It is also true you should run your newly created public company according to your long-term vision and not the immediate needs of the public equities marketplace. It may surprise you that this is easier to do than it might seem. Quarterly reporting of results is often regarded as the bane of long-term strategy, but it is also true that a quarter is usually the interval at which a company should be checking on its own performance anyway.

In the greater scheme, the right investors will find your company if your product or service benefits the commercial market. Your quarterly reporting makes those benefits visible to the world. And the results can be stunning. Ultimately, the company should be sold to those that have the founders' best interests at heart, which I maintain is the public markets. That's because it places a value on the company's vision and its ability to execute that vision. The market's goal is to maximize value, not minimize risk. This allows the business to be measured by the investments it makes and the risk it takes to grow and be (or become) profitable. The key then is to construct a business model that investors can believe in and the company can deliver. The market will maximize the company valuation if you deliver by making visible progress toward your promised business model.

That is a far better scenario than turning the fate of the company over to a group of VCs on your board whose sole interest is getting a quick return on their investment to mollify their investors, whose desires are paramount.

For all of these reasons, you need to consider going public through an initial offering of stock as part of your company's strategy. Indeed, failure to give this path close consideration would be a failure of your fiduciary responsibility to the company and a failure to provide the best possible future to your stakeholders . . . not least, yourself.

BATTLE SCARS

So of all the people who could advise you on your company's future, why should you listen to me? Well, the simple reason is that I probably have as much experience with IPOs over the last twenty years as anyone, particularly in high tech. In the process, I have learned to see them for what they are, stripped of all the myth and superstition. I have no illusions about what is required to achieve a successful IPO. Just as important, I understand the true role an IPO plays in the overall story of a company. Weekly, sometimes daily, people contact me for advice on going public. That's why I've created this book, a download of my best time-tested information and advice about going public.

Over the last two decades, I have been involved with three IPOs on the New York Stock Exchange as an executive and two more as a board member. None of these IPOs was easy—all required a lot of hard work, a willingness to jump on opportunities the moment they emerged, and a risk profile greater than most people are willing to accept. Indeed, I never took a job that others hadn't already looked at and assessed the risk as too high for them.

Let's face it, I did not wake up one day wanting to be a CFO. It was the furthest thing from my thoughts. Rather, I began sweeping floors at my parents' garage as a ten-year-old, running a paper route, and working at Longs Drugs. In college I took business classes, knowing that I could always do bookkeeping if other things did not work out. My first job out of college was working with a CPA firm. After two years and one day there, I knew I needed to look elsewhere for a career.

So I went to Indiana University and taught undergraduate accounting to pay for my MBA. Indiana was a great "get it done" university. The big-name schools are good, but even today, when I hire folks, I always look at what they got done—not where they went to school. Smart doesn't always mean accomplished. Indiana University taught me that.

After graduate school, in 1974, I was fortunate enough to get hired by the Santa Clara division of Hewlett-Packard, even then considered one of the world's best-managed companies. In the eighteen years I stayed with the company, it grew from $200 million to nearly $18 billion, and I was carried along in its success. Better yet, I met and worked with some wonderful people. Best of all, I had the chance to work for and learn from two of the greatest entrepreneurs in business history, Bill Hewlett and Dave Packard.

It was at HP where I learned to take on roles that nobody wanted and that provided a fast track to promotion for me. I discovered that there was almost no downside to those jobs; after all, nobody else wanted to try them, and I was expected to fail. When I didn't fail, I quickly rose through the ranks. In the process I learned leadership, planning, and execution. In time, I moved to the company's international business, spending nearly ten years in Asia, setting up HP's China, India, and Japan subsidiaries.

But it couldn't last forever. Bill and Dave retired, and the legendary "HP Way" of business began to fade. The free donuts and coffee and all the benefits and perks of the most enlightened company in history disappeared under a succession of new CEOs. Big-company politics filled the vacuum. My fellow employees understandably began to worry about their jobs and goals more than the company's success. I realized it was time to go.

I was recruited by the then-hottest new company in Silicon Valley, Silicon Graphics, to lead its international finance operations. At SGI, I further learned the ins and outs of international expansion. SGI also had the best employee support programs I have ever seen—not just in training, but in creating employee cohesion and improving morale. The company seemed to have an instinctual understanding that it takes team effort to achieve long-term success.

Personally, SGI helped build my self-confidence, giving me my first promotion to vice president. It was only then that I learned the tenuousness of that job title: there was no job security; if you didn't deliver consistently superior results, you were quickly replaced by someone else. That I survived only made me feel more confident.

Four years later, I approached Autodesk as they were looking for a new CFO. The recruiter looked at my resume and warned me that the CEO, Carol Bartz, wouldn't like me because I had no "C-level" experience. Luckily, nobody else wanted the job. My four years with Bartz, one of the most pioneering CEOs in the industry, were not only fun and rewarding, but, because Autodesk was a public company, they gave me my first experience dealing with Wall Street.

I might have stayed at Autodesk longer, but after four years, Marc Benioff approached me. Could I, he asked, recommend any candidates to be CFO of his start-up? At the time Salesforce was a little-known company that was going to put other companies' data in the cloud using a new technology called "utility computing" or software as a service (SaaS). After studying the company and its plans for a month, I decided to take a risk. I went back to Benioff and said, "Hey, why not me?"

With Marc's vision, we weren't starting just a new company, but a new industry. Leaving Autodesk was hard, but it was already an established company. I had come to learn that, in my heart, I was a *builder*—of teams, of systems, of businesses, and of new enterprises. I spent nine years at Salesforce, and it was perhaps the greatest experience of my working life. To start with a $20 million company in rented offices and see how it has grown to become a $17 billion global corporation headquartered in a skyscraper that towers over downtown San Francisco—what could match that?

But as companies grow, they change. My heart is always in new companies—their energy, optimism, and excitement. Salesforce had become a great, mature company, and I had been amply rewarded for helping it get there. It was time to move on. And so with Benioff's blessing, I retired.

After taking a few months off, I realized—like many before me—that you never really retire, you just move on to other experiences. I reentered the working world with a quick stop at a SaaS company in the sales compensation business called Xactly, and then I moved on to a much better-known company, Pandora.

Pandora was a new way to livestream music. For me, after having spent years in the enterprise computing industry, this was a chance to branch out and see if I could succeed in an Internet-based consumer business. It was a great choice: three years of hard work with a great finance team built from the ground up, and we took Pandora public in 2011.

Next came D-Wave Systems, a quantum computing company based in Vancouver. Quantum computers will change the world someday, and D-Wave is the real deal. I learned something important at the company: there is a right size and state of a new company, and that is where I can add value in the ramp-up to an IPO. I was there too early, and my operation was just a drag on the company's limited resources.

So after two years at D-Wave, I launched off again, this time looking for a tech start-up in New York City. Why there? Because, having lived and worked in San Francisco most of my career, I thought a change would be good. I found what I was looking for—Yext, a $50 million company with a great founder and CEO, Howard Lerman; a terrific team; and the chance, once again, to build not only a company, but a whole industry.

I'll tell more of the Yext story later. For now, it's enough to know that we took Yext public on the New York Stock Exchange in April 2017.

Why am I telling you my life story, other than to prove my bona fides and give you a glimpse of the peripatetic life of a CFO specializing in IPOs? Note the companies where I've worked—several features stand out.

First, the range of these enterprises: their businesses reach across the tech spectrum. I daresay that if, instead of electronics, my focus had been on some other vertical—manufacturing, consumer products, tourism and hospitality, or any number of different industries—my resume would be just as eventful, suggesting that IPOs are possible in whatever business you are in.

Second, after HP, the companies I've just described cover the last two decades. In other words, they successfully went public precisely during the years when doing so was seen as passé or even career poison. In fact, they thrived on the experience, raised the money they needed to continue growing, and—as the numbers show—came out better for the experience.

Third, and I think most importantly, they are still here. How many other firms founded at the same time and in the same industry have survived? How many are gone? Perhaps 90 percent? The process of preparing for the IPO streamlined these companies, put in place systems that guided them through their next phase, and rationalized their business process, and then the IPO provided them with the capital they need to survive subsequent hard economic times and to invest during good times.

Finally—and I speak selfishly—I can look back on those years and those companies with great pride, because those businesses are still there to remind me of the hard work by my teams and me. Just as the assembly line guy who works at the Ford River Rouge plant can say about the passing Galaxies and Mustangs, I can point those companies out to my children—and one day my grandchildren—and proudly say, "I helped build that." Today, when most resumes are filled with the names of companies that have been acquired or merged away or simply extinguished, how many people can say the same?

THE PATH

I hope that I have, if not fully convinced you of the value of pursuing an IPO at your company, at least intrigued you and challenged you to consider the possibility. At the start of this book and in the chapters that follow, I present the steps you need to take, before and after going public day, to become a successful, publicly traded corporation.

Along the way, I'll share with you some of my own experiences, point out some pitfalls, share some tricks, and provide you with other sources for support and advice. In the appendix you will find a timeline and road map for tasks to complete before the IPO. Hopefully, with ongoing review, this will help you achieve your goal.

Going public isn't easy; but it can be exhilarating. And when that magical day arrives, you'll know that you have made history. How often does that happen in one's career?

Now, let's start down that path. It all begins with a decision . . .

CHAPTER 1

THE DECISION TO GO PUBLIC

A company's decision to go public typically originates in conversations among members of the board of directors or senior management. The conversation may emerge through other topics, such as the need to raise cash for the company to continue to grow, the challenge of competing against lower pricing by a new cohort of competing start-ups, the founders' impatience after years of hard work going unrewarded, or the underlying venture capital (VC) investor's fund approaching its maturity and liquidation event. Wherever the conversations start, they coalesce into a single question:

Do we sell the company or do we go public?

Needless to say, the people involved in these conversations have different perspectives and agendas, and not all of those agendas support the near-term or long-term best interests of the company. (For example, impatience and greed are terrible reasons to make a business decision.) When cooler heads prevail, the real question becomes:

> *Do we want to walk away from what we've built, or do*
> *we want to develop a business with a lasting future?*

Though I hold strongly that a successful company should choose to go public, I also agree with skeptics: going public and subsequently running a publicly traded company is a lot of work. So now the question becomes:

> *Do you want to put in the work?*

Some founder teams and investors are clear on this point: they don't want to take on the job of transforming their company, nor do they want to entrust their gains to the people they will need to hire to replace them. No matter the potential benefits for their professional legacies, their stakeholders, or the company's reach, they want to take their winnings and leave the table. If that's what you want to do, okay. End of story. Put the book down and walk away.

As for everybody else—those of you who want to build a company that lasts and share its success with all your current and future stakeholders—congratulations! You've made an exciting decision. Years from now you will look back at this choice with satisfaction. But for now, it's time to kick off a project that will take a couple years to reach fruition, with repercussions that may last decades: preparing your company, both structurally and financially, to go public.

In this chapter, we will look at the first steps along the path to going public, which you take when IPO day is still a far-off event, twenty-four months or more away. Many of the decisions described here might seem minor, even arbitrary, but their long-term impacts will be profound.

FIND A "REAL CFO"

By the time most enterprises have decided to go public, they already have someone who wears the title CFO. But in reality, in a private start-up this person is doing the job of a business manager. There's nothing wrong with that. On the contrary, outside of the chief scientist, the business manager is often the most important employee in a new start-up on a day-to-day basis, exceeding even the value of the CEO.

Why? Because, in the words of Alan Shugart, Founder of Shugart Associates and Seagate Technology, "Cash flow is more important than your mother." Few start-ups ever succeed out of the gate with their first product idea. Rather, they need time to revise their offering to fit an emerging market. Most companies don't have that time, because they run out of money . . . and die. A business manager who can run a lean, financially disciplined company is often the best hope a start-up has of making it out of the gate.

Unfortunately, these individuals, for all of their admirable gifts, have more experience saving companies from doom than growing them, and few, if any, know how to prepare a company to go public. There's no room for a business-managing CFO to gain that experience along the way to an IPO; there is just too much at stake.

I have nothing but respect for those professionals who suffer through the early days of a start-up as they struggle to keep it solvent. Similarly, I'm in awe of those CFOs who manage vast departments dedicated to providing strong financial underpinnings to multi-billion-dollar Fortune 500 companies. But when you're going public, those aren't the talent sets you need.

This is where people like me come in. My sweet spot—one I share with a number of financial veterans in the tech industry—is structuring a company to go public, taking it through that transformation, and then setting it on its way into the future. This process includes finding the next person who wants a career running the processes I put in place.

Of course, finding the right CFO to bridge your company into an IPO is not as simple as posting a job listing. You need to prepare your company to attract the talent you want. How do you do that? Let me tell you how it looks from my perspective.

First of all, CFOs versed in taking companies public are looking for businesses that have a strong identity and sense of purpose. CFOs are wary of businesses that don't really know who they are, what they want, or how to get there. Often these companies don't understand why or even when they have a great product. For the same reason they can't find venture capital money, they won't attract a skilled CFO to take them public: without even knowing it, they are setting off warning alarms for the person across the table.

I've learned to see future trouble long before a company even suspects it. Time, experience, and a trustworthy intuition make people in my role extremely selective. After all, if I'm going to devote months, even years, of my life to this company, I'm going to have to be pretty damn sure I can help it be successful.

For me, involvement with a young company thinking of going public begins with an e-mail via LinkedIn, asking if I would be interested in participating in such an initiative. Usually, after some quick research on the company, my response is "No, thank you." But if the start-up captures my interest, I may ask for some basic information, such as where the company is located (because I will have to move there; this is not a job done remotely), what its current revenue is (that is, does the company even approach the threshold of an IPO?), and what industry they are in (an emerging industry may not yet find the stock market receptive; a mature industry may not offer enough upside).

By the way, a note on location: often companies desperately searching for pre-IPO leadership settle for executive hires even when the executive refuses to move to the company's location and instead wants to work remotely with ongoing trips to headquarters. It may sound good, but it is in fact a pipe dream for both parties. There are several reasons for this.

First, your CFO needs to build a finance team. That is very hard to pull off if you are a mail-order CFO. You need at least two to three years—on the ground and full-time—to get the basic team in place and working harmoniously.

Second, the CFO needs to also become part of the senior management team. That can only happen with in-person presence, not through e-mails and conference calls. Values, common language, and direction are established through ongoing conversations, and if your CFO is not part of the conversation, your CFO will not be part of the direction setting.

Finally, for the company, there are many decisions, directions, and behavioral changes to be made. Not having a senior executive present makes this very difficult. Now, it is true that as the company grows and scales you need to transition to a more remote management practice.

But by then, you should have the values and language in place. That's when you may need your executives at headquarters or near major customers, with employees (and some team members) scattered at new offices around the world. For now though, your CFO needs to be close to home.

Okay, back to initial inquiries with young companies. Needless to say, much of the information I ask for before considering a CFO position is confidential, so the company may be unwilling to share. If that's the case, I restate my lack of interest and move forward. However, on those occasions where something about the company or its business jumps out at me, I may follow up with the recruiter to learn more about the opportunity.

Funny, when I do sit down with the recruiter, it is always the same sales pattern:

- The company revenues are rapidly growing at more than 100 percent year over year, which means it had only $2 million in revenue last year.
- It is a leader in its market space, meaning as yet there are no competitors, but they are coming fast.
- It is looking to go public in eighteen to twenty-four months— that is, they are not sure yet about an IPO.

By the way, if the recruiter says the company is planning an IPO in less than nine months, I am immediately on guard. It takes at least eighteen months to get ready for an IPO. Inside that window, it can be done, but the risk profile jumps dramatically. As the CFO and CEO personally will be on the hook for any misstatements, misreported financials, or other misdeeds—you know, the stuff that happens when you are trying to rush an IPO—I know I will be liable. That's why, when I hear a figure like nine months, I know it's time to run away, unless the board is willing to consider a more reasonable time frame.

Now, let's say that I haven't been scared off by the recruiter but instead have heard enough good things to be intrigued by the company's vision, business plans, and competitive situation. The next step is to meet the company's management, because in the end, personal chemistry matters.

At the same time, I'll want to have discussions with board members, read media coverage of the company, and talk to the company's biggest investors.

Regarding the last group of individuals: as powerful and influential as they may be, remember that, while they have a financial interest, they rarely have an operating interest in the company. Most, if not all, will not be involved with the company after the IPO. Primarily I am interested to see how they will support, distort, or impede the going-public process. For a prospective CFO, a difficult investor can make life miserable. This is especially true when the investor's motives are antithetical to the company's interests. It might be someone who wants an immediate drive to profitability or a cash-flow-positive event for his or her own needs instead of those of the company. Indeed, that person's presence can be a deal breaker for me.

I worked with one start-up that needed additional funding and brought in two more VCs to provide the cash. The first thing these VCs did was suggest the company cut spending by reducing the number of sales reps by half and by moving development to India. These moves would have been disastrous. A growing company needs a growing sales and distribution operation, not a diminishing one. This is one department where efficiency typically becomes less efficient by cutting.

Similarly, at such a critical time in the company's story, moving development to reduce costs inevitably extends development cycles and moves the developers further away from customer feedback.

Eventually, I left that company. On the way out, I suggested they use my compensation to retain their sales reps. The company eventually went public, but within two years it was acquired by a private equity firm. The painful truth is the company failed to achieve a significant volume of business, in part because of lack of distribution. Those new VCs sabotaged the company instead of helping it succeed. Their money proved to be too expensive.

What does all this mean to you as you're looking for the type of CFO you'll need to take your company public?

You can expect a CFO candidate to conduct their due diligence. So be prepared to open your books, to be honest about your business and leadership teams' weaknesses, and to make the important people in your organization available for meetings.

The reviews and discussions you have while recruiting a CFO can become the foundation for future success.

Let's say that your company has survived a CFO candidate's investigative process, shows great potential for a successful IPO, and is willing to do the hard work to get there. You've successfully negotiated an employment contract with your new CFO that includes both salary and stock options. (You'll want to offer the latter to ensure that the CFO has skin in the game.) Now, the process of preparing to go public officially begins.

Now let's look at the very first steps on that path, which involve getting all of the stakeholders on board.

CHAPTER 2

ALL ABOARD

How do you get all the key players involved in your company to agree on going public? Let's walk through the various topics that will require consensus from both the board of directors and senior management.

ASSESS THE CASH NEEDS OF THE COMPANY

This will determine whether the company is ready to move toward that IPO immediately or if it needs to find a cash injection first. Among the questions to ask: What is the monthly burn rate? Why is it so? What ideas do the board or management have to reduce cash burn? Which (if any) of the investors is willing to provide additional funds to help the company get to the IPO date?

In the early days of the Internet, I was asked to interview with the now-infamous Pets.com. I loved the leadership, the location was in downtown San Francisco, you could bring your dog to work, and everyone was on a mission to change how we purchase pet items, most notably pet food. I spent the day meeting management and some of the

VC investors and touring the facility. It was all very cool, and I began to imagine myself being part of the company's future.

But, as I was walking out of the warehouse, I casually asked, "How do you sell pet food at below cost, and how do you intend to cover those costs and the resulting negative cash flow?"

My guide, who happened to be the CEO, replied, "Increased volume, become more efficient in other areas, and use pet food as the loss leader." That sounded good at first. But as I began to ponder that answer, it reminded of the punch line to the old joke, "Sure, we're losing money on every sale, but we'll make it up in volume!"

Pets.com's fatal flaw was that an overwhelming fraction of the company's revenue was pet food sales, the enterprise's loss leader. It would be very difficult to find other synergies to make the business profitable.

So in the end, I passed on working with some great individuals and quality VCs. Everyone knows what happened next: Pets.com never did make a profit. Its death was one of the most spectacular of the dot-com bust. That said, it laid the foundation for online web sales in the pet category. The decision to rely on the food category was Pets.com's issue. Expanding to higher-margin products or a unique pet food, such as Blue Mountain provided, would have allowed for higher-margin business while reducing the losses created by the loss leader product. The focus might have been on convenience of order and delivery rather than "cheaper than your local pet shop."

At the end of the day, the most important metric in running a business, any business, is cash generation. Even the unicorns, as they are known, eventually went public because they needed cash. The public investor's valuation includes timing to positive cash flow. It is not enough to say you will be cash flow positive; you must get cash flow positive. So that is the number one item I focus on when working with start-ups. Cash is king and always will be. Many public investors use a discounted cash flow model to determine your company's valuation. So pay attention to this critical process of generating positive cash flow.

OWNERSHIP

If, with your new CFO's help, your company does conclude that it will not be able to make it through the eighteen months to the IPO without more cash, this is the time to search for another VC, even if it means surrendering more of the company's ownership (though at least at a higher valuation), or offering that VC a board position.

But proceed with caution.

In my experience, bringing in a new investor sounds good on paper, but it can become a disaster in practice. Sure, everybody gets a little something. Management gets some liquidity, the company gets some cash, and existing VCs may sell some of their shares to the new VC. At this point the company usually has a lot of shares to sell. They are going to be offered up in the IPO anyway, so why not make money off them now?

But here is the rub: with a new investor in the company, the valuation increases, but only because the added cash has increased the value of the company. Or did it? Perversely, especially if the company isn't financially disciplined, your monthly cash burn may in fact go up, so the value of your assets may actually depreciate quickly.

Moreover, significant dilution may have happened to everyone involved with the company (that is, except for the VCs who managed to get anti-dilution privileges written into their original purchase agreements). Those who do not have anti-dilution clauses get even more diluted. Typically they are folks, including founders and existing executives and employees, who have done the hard work of getting the company to this point. Understandably, this dilution can leave a bitter taste in their mouths.

The founder of the company is often the most affected by this late investment. He or she rightly begins with a very large percentage of the company. But every round of financing reduces the amount of that ownership—often by a lot. One team I worked with ended up with less than 20 percent of the ownership interest in the company; and the founder, who began with 50 percent, ended up with just 8 percent. Thus, by the final reckoning at the IPO, the VCs owned 65 percent of the stock, the founder 20 percent, and the employees just 15 percent. In other words, those who owned 35 percent of the company were creating the wealth for the people who owned 65 percent. That's a disappointing result for the founders and employees who worked so hard to create and increase the value of the company.

On the flip side, I know a savvy founder who owned 100 percent of his company. He got the company off the ground with an initial fundraise that reduced his ownership to 65 percent, but in doing so, he also demanded and received higher valuations for his founding idea for the company. In addition, he obtained an anti-dilution clause in all future funding. Further, he looked to friends and family to fill the initial rounds that got the company's product to proof of concept. Finally, he put into place a business model that generated cash up front. And that enabled him, from then on, never again to look to VCs for funding, or to dilute his or his employees' efforts.

Now, not everyone is so fortunate to have friends and family who can back their company financially. But building a real business does not always require selling everything up front to venture investors. It is possible—for example, through anti-dilution clauses and cash-up-front business models—to ensure that founders and employees, the folks who actually create the value of the business, get their fair share of returns for the effort they put into the business.

SUSTAINABILITY

If the business model for a company has no plan, over time, to achieve cash flow break-even or positive cash flow, it is likely not a sustainable business. This is true even for large capital expenditure businesses, the only difference being that the time horizons are longer. But whatever the time horizon, every company needs a vision and a model for execution to get to cash flow positive. This is the first challenge to sustainability: you need a viable model.

Neither the private nor public markets are made up of infinite cash to fund businesses. Going public gives you ongoing access to a very efficient and practical source of capital, one that will continuously assess the risk to determine the cost of that capital and progress toward your planned business model. Thus, share dilution and capital-raise costs become more tied to the view of the business's current and future needs and growth of the business, rather than on who can get the biggest stake in the company. With analysts and public shareholders, you now have a real sounding board—not just solitary, isolated, and often biased investors.

The second challenge to sustainability has to do with your venture investors and their time constraints. Each VC invests through funds they have put together via limited-partner investors (LPs) in the fund. The funds typically have a ten-year duration, at which point distributions are made to their investors.

If you have venture investors putting money in your company from newly formed funds, they may have a ten-year window before they have to generate liquidity. On the other hand, if you have a venture investor whose fund is already into its fifth or sixth year, it will compel the investor to either push your company public or to look for other venture investors to buy out their shares. Either way it will create an unwelcome time pressure. By the same token, should you be in a space where your venture investors have been invested in the company for five to seven years or longer, regardless of your business, that money is going to become impatient, and some liquidity event is going to have to happen.

When that deadline approaches, to maintain sustainability, every company should have three scenarios in development, in order of desirability:

- Plan A: IPO
- Plan B: Find another VC to invest in the company, preferably buying shares from the retiring VC's aging fund (preferably at a higher valuation than originally invested to show a return to the LPs)
- Plan C: Find that bigger company to sell out to

Experience has taught me that, left to their own devices, neither the management team nor the venture investors will ever sort this out or make a full commitment to any of these three scenarios until the day before the IPO or acquisition. Instead they'll engage in endless debates about the real value of the company—not least because there is no trustworthy or objective metric available to determine it. Every player in the debate will come from their own biases and expectations, arguing for a lower or higher valuation.

Unfortunately, these valuations are rarely tied to public market valuations. So on IPO day they run the risk of lower valuation by the public market, consequently disappointing late stage investors. Or they push the IPO price too high and disappoint public company investors as the price falls rather than rises after IPO.

Instead of allowing venture investors to determine fictional values that show returns on their portfolio, why not use the public markets to set the real value of the company?

In fact, even if you choose to sell to a bigger company, one of the best ways to get a premium valuation on your company is to go public and use that price point as your opening position in the merger negotiations. Take for example a company called MindBody. It went public and remained so for about two years, at which point it was sold to a private equity firm at more than 60 percent premium over its value on the public market. While I am not a big advocate for selling your business at all, a 60-plus percent premium is not bad.

As you can see, it is easy to get diverted by the lure of an immediate payout or desperation for a safe harbor and choose to sell out—when the best option is to stay the course and become a mature, public company. In the end, it often comes down to leadership: the CEO must have the confidence and maturity to stand for what is best for the company against all forces pursuing their own agendas.

PUBLIC OR PRIVATE?

This is a big one. Once the company decides it wants to go public, and searches neither for another round of investment nor for a buy-out, the principal players must answer one question:

*Is the company ready to make the investments in time
and money to prepare itself to go public?*

While it may seem odd to ask this question after the decision to proceed to go public, this is when the reality of the decision and desires for an IPO finally meet and form a single path to IPO.

In other words, is the company willing to devote the resources to build a real business, with internal reporting systems, experienced executives, and an investment in sales and marketing, to be able, ultimately, to go public? Without that commitment, going public is merely a pipe dream.

Say your company has between $50 million and $80 million in revenue, your growth rate is in the 40-plus percent range, if not higher, and you can see $100 million in revenue within two years, as well as a growing addressable market. At this size and stage, you really ought to get committed to the public markets, build the infrastructure, make the management hires, and take other actions to prepare to go public.

Are you ready to make that commitment? Needless to say, answering this question first requires answering a series of smaller questions:

Does the company currently have the ability to sustain a ten- to fifteen-year growth plan?

What size is the market, and how big a share can be captured by the company with its current business model?

The public market is looking for companies that can achieve up to $1 billion in market capital and have a longer run potential to grow that valuation significantly. Does the company have the potential to achieve a $1 billion revenue run rate, profitability, and cash flow break-even within a five- to ten-year window from IPO?

Remember when I said the very act of preparing for an IPO is a valuable disciplining process for a company? Now do you see what I mean? These are challenging hurdles, but you can clear them, and your company will be better for it.

By the way, I am not suggesting that all of the company's potential revenue will come from organic growth. That would be great until a company passes the $300 to $500 million mark in revenue, but it is just as likely that it will look to mergers and acquisitions to help carry it through and beyond the $1 billion revenue mark. That possibility should be in your plans as well.

What is often lost in the burden of day-to-day operations is the big picture, the context. This is the moment, eighteen to twenty-four months out from a potential IPO, when you should set aside time to reflect on who you are as a company, how far you have come, and where you want to go.

The fact is, you're having these conversations about an IPO because you have founded a viable business, successfully grown it, and are now on the threshold of joining the ranks of great companies. In order to continue to grow and succeed, you need capital, both financial and human. That is the essence of a business.

At the end of the day, you could run a very successful private business and never go public. Unfortunately, this is an unlikely strategy if you have taken on venture investors. Still, it can be done. My own family has built a business with a globally recognized brand and image, in wines (which is why you may have recognized my surname). There were no VCs involved. Yes, the family took on some bank debt, but generally the winery grew, thanks to good business folks with a practical sense for building a company from the ground up. They had a great product, focused on one-to-one selling (a tasting room) to create a tipping point, and followed that with a unique go-to-market strategy. In addition to that acumen, success required an ongoing dedication by the family to make it all work and to change as the business grew.

That said, Cakebread Cellars is run as if it is a public company. It has an outside board of directors and a great management team that can operate the day-to-day, while still thinking long term. It manages, with information from its reporting and monitoring systems, to know when things are going well and when they are not. The company manages various channels of distribution and the associated margins within those channels, it uses debt for its necessary capital purchases while maintaining a firm hand on payback and return on investment, and it has independent auditors and tax advisors.

My point here is not to cheerlead my family business. I simply want to remind you that if your company (whether public or private) is going to succeed, eventually you have to run a business with all the trimmings and overhead that come with it. For sure the family business does not carry the weight of having the SEC constantly looking over its shoulder, but it does carry other forms of government reporting and review requirements: the ATF (Bureau of Alcohol, Tobacco, Firearms, and Explosives), state boards that control distribution, local taxes, and other regulators. In other words, one should not think for a minute that a private business is without regulated overhead.

I'll go even further: when it comes to all the government paperwork, it may be easier and cheaper to be a public company. How is that even possible? Because most public companies of $100 million or more in revenue can enjoy a valuation in the $1 billion-plus range in market value, if they provide significant revenue growth in their early years from IPO. Thus, they can invest something in the area of $5 to $10 million in additional administrative controls and the staff to manage them. So while the regulatory burden may be greater on a public company, dealing with regulations may put proportionately less demand on a public company than on a private one.

PRICING

This may seem wildly premature, but this is the point when you should begin your preliminary investigations into how much money you want to raise, which in turn will lead to calculations of how many shares you want to put on the market, and thus, what your opening stock price will need to be.

You don't need to come to any final conclusions yet. But you should be doing this calculation—and undertaking comparisons with comparable companies—starting about two years ahead of your planned IPO. This will ensure that you book the proper stock compensation expense and have properly valued the stock options you are granting.

FINDING AND RETAINING TALENT

A final thought: discussions of your company's future must consider the fate of current employees and the near-term ability to recruit new top talent. Yes, some employees care only about cash, not long-term career opportunities. That is especially true for young college recruits. But a successful start-up, as it transforms into a sustainable company, needs a mix of talent at all experience levels, and some of that older talent is very much interested in their careers. To recruit this type of talent requires pre-IPO stock options. Most seasoned people are likely to be on their second or third start-up, so they well know the value and upside of those options. If you are going to grow from a start-up to a highly successful company, you need these people, and the ability to offer pre-IPO stock options will help you recruit them.

As you grow, you also need to hire executives, managers, and employees who have worked at larger organizations and who know the potholes that lie ahead. They are the key to both a successful and stable workforce and to building a company that can thread its way through the minefield of growing to greatness. To attract those individuals, you will need to offer stock packages of either stock options or restricted stock units (RSUs).

Tellingly, an IPO, because of the media attention it receives and the resulting brief penumbra of success that surrounds the company, can be a valuable tool in attracting this top senior talent. Moreover, these folks, because they tend to have a lower risk-taking threshold, often see your having gone public as just the kind of financial security they need to make the leap. Furthermore, these folks are often pricey, so without a public offering you will find it even more difficult to recruit them, as they need the monetary upside in their cash and stock employment package. Rarely would someone with this type of management experience join a pre-IPO company, because the risk of business failure is too high. An IPO, in essence, can help validate your business and its long-term future success.

A DEFINING DECISION

Even if you decide that now is not the right time to work toward an IPO, the process of making that decision can be salutary. Companies, and especially start-ups, tend to devolve into a focus on short-term results and current economics. The very act of discussing a potential IPO forces the company to, at least temporarily, shift its focus to the long-term and questions of sustainability.

That said, as you start the process of going public, beware of the "safe" solution of going outside the company for professional advice. Advisors, such as lawyers, accountants, and bankers, have their place, but their agendas are different from the company's. You want to do what is best for your company; they want to earn a big fee. So what do you think they will advise you to do? Why, go public—of course! And, of course, pay their bills promptly.

If you feel the need for some outside points of view, or at least to hear some new perspectives, by all means bring in the experts. But don't feel obliged to follow their advice. This is your company, built on your blood, sweat, and tears. Ultimately, its fate is for you to decide. Unlike those advisors, you have a lot to gain and a lot to lose. You're the one who understands the gravity of your decision, and that degree of seriousness cannot be bought.

CHAPTER 3

ASSESSMENT

Okay, you're ready to attract a CFO who will help the company go public, and your stakeholders have come to a consensus about cash flow, sustainability, and infrastructure. Now, you're eighteen to twenty-four months away from IPO. You've got a lot—sometimes it will feel like too much—to do between now and then, but don't worry. In the following chapters, I'll walk you through the steps to get there.

We'll begin with the assessment process, which will run in parallel with the hiring of the CFO and his or her team.

The assessment process, often neglected, is actually critical to positioning a company for going public. (By the way, if you are considering stepping into a pre-IPO role at a company, you should do some of this assessment before you take the job.)

ASSESSING YOUR TEAMS

You will notice that some of the recommended areas for assessment listed below will represent big changes for your company in the future. That said, no one area is more important than the others. You must complete all of them to set an effective path toward your IPO. Let's look at each in turn.

1. Understand the Business Model and Drivers of Revenue, Cash, and Profitability

The business model impacts so much of how the company should be run that it really needs to be an early area of focus.

Let me describe what I mean by business model, as the term has multiple definitions in the business world.

Most businesses have a few ways to look at their operations. Personally, I think you need at least three perspectives to obtain a full view. For the business model, first I typically look at the high-level income statement and cash flow from operations.

Second, I look at what the company currently is doing in terms of revenue growth and gross margins after cost of sales.

Third, I look at specific components of operating spend.

The last I divide into cost of sales, marketing, research and development (or product development), general, and administrative.

When assessing the business model, I recommend you look at two components. The first is year-over-year revenue growth. The second is spend-as-a-percentage-of-revenue. These metrics can help you determine if you might be over- or underinvesting in a component of your business. Looking out over ten years, devise a business model you want to achieve and use these metrics to check the company's progress.

2. Understand the Details of Your COGS

Identifying the components of your cost of goods sold (COGS) is also important, as it determines your gross margins. Note that the components of COGS are generally defined by the industry you are in, not by generally accepted accounting principles (GAAP). For that reason, I have no specific guidance on what you should include in the COGS category for your company. Instead, I recommend looking to your peer industry group (more on that soon) to see what your competitors are doing for COGS, while remaining mindful about what makes the most sense for your company. I can tell you that your COGS generally reflect the margins made on an item sold. Note as well that it also sets the basis for what you can spend in the other functional categories and remain profitable. So be thoughtful, be consistent over time, and make sure you can associate each cost element with a product or service you are delivering to your customer.

The other functions of a business are just as meaningful to building your business model. Sales and marketing, for example, obviously are critical to a company's success. By marketing, I mean efforts to raise product and company awareness, lead-generation activities, and over time, brand awareness. Now, each industry has distinct parameters of success. For example, in the software and Internet space, I think spending 11 to 13 percent of revenue on marketing is appropriate. This may be different for your industry. So if you find your sales and marketing spending is significantly higher or lower than your peer group's, you need to appreciate the implications over time of this ratio of revenue to spend.

3. Pick Your Peer Group Wisely

Yes, you're going to need to assess your company against your peer group.

Don't be shy: call and develop a relationship with your peer group companies to get a better understanding of how they may be doing things. Not all peer companies are direct competitors, and even if they are there is value in getting to know them.

In this area of assessment, it's important to select your peer group companies carefully, as your selections will help establish your baseline in your execution against those competitors. In dealings with outside investors, this will help ensure you are successfully performing against your peer group in each category of spend, gross margin, and profitability. In setting up peer groups, I look back to companies that may have similar business models but are more mature, with ten, fifteen, or even twenty years in the market.

That said, context is important when comparing your company against this peer group. It was amazing to me, in the early days of Salesforce, that Wall Street was so concerned when we were running losses. They consistently compared our customer relationship management (CRM) service with those of Microsoft, Oracle, SAP, Autodesk, and other mature software companies. It drove me crazy, because those investors were comparing metrics of a start-up with companies that had been in business for well over a decade. It was apples and oranges. Microsoft, SAP, and Autodesk were already fifteen to twenty years into their businesses, and they were selling software packages, not SaaS. The annual growth rates of those older, bigger companies had slowed to less than 5 percent—so of course they should have been generating huge net margins of between 30 and 40 percent of revenue. If you went back to each of those companies and looked at their first five years and then the five years after IPO, Salesforce ranked in the middle or better.

In context, comparison to your peers will help you improve your operations. It may even suggest you have found a better way to execute than your peer group.

That said, these comparisons are fraught with issues, particularly in the area of allocation of costs. Consider the following questions:

- Are facilities costs allocated on head count or occupied square footage of the function?
- How are other facilities charged when not all functions reside in that facility?
- How are the costs of IT resources allocated—by head count or some other metric?
- How does the company treat bad debt write-offs (for example, a charge to administration or a charge to sales)?

The variables in these allocations can make comparisons to peers more challenging. Despite these variables, at the end of the day, the overall comparison still will let you know whether or not you are in the game.

Build your business model, know where you are today, and get some clarity on where you need to be in five to ten years to drive the valuation of your company in a public market. This also means you need to understand how the market will value your company. Is it revenue growth; net income growth; earnings before interest, tax, depreciation, and amortization (EBITDA) growth; or some other metric?

One thing for sure: look to cash flow growth as a valuation metric regardless of your business. Either free cash flow (FCF), which includes capital spend, or operating cash flow (OCF) if you are a software or services company.

4. Know Your Sales Team's Capabilities

Assess the quality of the company's employees. All functions matter, of course, but one area that bites many companies is the sales organization. The product teams and the sales and services teams are critical. I'm talking about the people who bring in the deals and the people who support both the pre- and post-sales situations. Generally, early sales leadership is capable of getting the company to about $100 million, perhaps $200 million, but to scale a sales organization to achieve $1 billion in revenues takes sophisticated processes, specifically understanding the customer and sales support functions to ensure that customers receive what they have been sold.

Look at this multifunction organization very carefully and be open to an honest assessment about how it needs to change as the business scales. Who has worked at larger companies, for example? Who has built processes and scaled them? Who can communicate with larger groups of people? These are all skills to consider as you assess the team. The result of this assessment is knowing which individuals you will need to replace and when.

At Salesforce, Marc Benioff made some brilliant and long-lasting decisions regarding the sales organization. First, he split the organization into "enterprise direct selling" and "mid-market / small business tele-selling" (but still direct to the customer). For the latter group he put a team in place and hired someone as its sales leader who had experience developing the processes necessary to scale in this market. He also had the sales leader report directly to him.

At the same time, Benioff brought in industry veterans who had worked at multi-billion-dollar tech companies in the enterprise direct space to start and grow that business. It worked because these executives came with great business skills, knew the playbook for addressing customer needs, could hire experienced direct sales executives, and knew how to work with sales administrators to set up the processes and practices to scale the business worldwide. As it turns out, "been there, done that" is not a bad thing in scaling an enterprise sales force.

Time and again, newly public companies stumble because at some point they have to change out the sales leadership when it proves unable to scale. This typically slows revenue growth, frustrates investors, and slows or reduces valuations until the company can get back on track, which is usually a two-year process. So the smart strategy is to anticipate this moment, figure out your transition timings for your key roles, and get started pre-IPO so your transitions are complete before that critical time.

At Yext, we started this transition at the time we went public. Our timing was good for the long-term health of the company, but it was too late for our investors' comfort. Ultimately it paid off, but it would have been much smoother had we executed earlier. It's a reminder that you always need to be looking at the future and to the changes you will need to make to sustain growth.

5. Build Your Finance and Legal Team for the Future

Another critical part of this process is putting into place a long-term finance and legal team. After all, this team will bear the brunt of the work to prepare the company to go public and then keep the process going post-IPO. Once the CFO is on board and understands the capabilities of the finance and legal team, the CFO needs to upgrade and hire team members to help grow the business.

This group needs to have a variety of skills. At the very least, the members need a technical understanding of accounting and internal controls. They don't have to read accounting journals in their free time, but they must have a strong fundamental knowledge of accounting principles. While folks typically look to public accounting firms to provide this type of talent, the fact is that audit work is not corporate accounting work, so I typically look for veteran public accountants from corporate accounting departments.

Every transaction and process the team members establish must reflect proper accounting. If this basic knowledge is missing, you will never get the financials correct, and you will run the high risk of financial restatements. You most assuredly do not want that—last-minute restatements have killed more than one IPO.

One other note: don't even consider hiring candidates who want to join your company one or even two years into their professional careers. I was one of those who went into public accounting out of school, lasted two years and one day at one of the big CPA firms, and was let go. As a result, though I have a nice resume item early in my career, back then I had no more idea of debits and credits than the man on the moon. Had I stayed any longer, my career in corporate accounting would have come to a quick end.

Instead I pursued an MBA in international business and corporate finance. I then taught undergrad accounting to pay the bills and learned enough in the process to graduate actually knowing what corporate accounting was and how to be successful at it. Looking back, I also made another important decision: not to go into investment banking. I preferred creating real, tangible value. The point is, look for people on their second or third job, not folks out of school, as often they are not aware of the demands of the job.

What you do need to do—about nine months before going public—is to hire an SEC reporting specialist. This person needs to live, breathe, and enjoy SEC and GAAP accounting pronouncements, but also to be able to communicate with the management and the rest of the accounting department. Really great folks in this area are hard to find. Networking with public accounting firms, other CFOs, investment bankers, and legal counsel can help source this role. The effort to find the right person will pay off, because they play a critical role in getting SEC filings completed. This role needs to be combined with a legal person who is equally well focused on SEC filings.

Keep in mind that your team needs to be skillful at the basics and should include a payroll specialist, an accounts payable expert, a general ledger accountant, a fixed asset accountant, and someone to help with the closing process. This last specialist gets the books closed on a five- to seven-day schedule. You can't go public and take thirty days to close the books and report your SEC filings.

Thus, one major condition for going public is the ability to achieve a seven-day close and take not more than ten days from month end to get your financial statements completed. Remember: it takes auditors at least two weeks to review the financials, so your ten days to close and their ten days to review does not leave much time to complete the SEC paperwork and get your information ready for an earnings call.

6. Organize Your Billings and Accounts Receivable Teams

The other groups that need your attention are the billings team and the accounts receivable (AR) team. This is the real beginning of the process of invoicing customers, recording revenue, and collecting cash. Getting a contract from a customer does nothing to enhance the value of the company unless you can invoice the customer and subsequently get paid.

That sounds pretty basic, right? Yet when I joined Yext, it was taking two to four weeks to invoice a customer, and then we just hoped that customer would pay us. Meanwhile, no one really was looking at past due balances. These two processes are critical and yet severely under-resourced at most companies. The bottom line, literally, is that you must be able to invoice a customer the same or next day as a contract is signed or products and services are delivered. A longer cycle time dramatically impacts the business.

Frankly, forget about being a public company; why would you run any business that invoices customers a month later? Think of this in terms of a restaurant having a customer enjoy a great meal and then walk out of the door saying, "Send me the bill." Having provided all of the labor, materials, service, and assets to prepare a great meal, why would you have your customer pay for it at a later date? The meal certainly will never be returned and resold. The point is, providing a service or product should immediately result in revenue recognition and timely payment. Again, this is Business 101 and has nothing particularly to do with going public, but it is another process that must be in place when you do go public.

The other aspect of this assessment is your AR and collections process. This is yet another business basic that must be covered, whether you are public or not. A simple investment in a credit and collections person or two makes a world of difference when it comes to achieving positive cash flow.

One of the first hires I typically make is a credit and collections person. The mere act of hiring such an individual will often reduce accounts receivable balances dramatically. At all three companies that I took public, we moved days sales outstanding (DSO) from approximately ninety days to an average of fifty-five days or fewer. That's almost a 50 percent improvement in the timing of payments, which means we had access to that money more than a month earlier. Sure, for the most part customers will pay you, eventually, but getting them all to pay in thirty days is one of the best ways to improve cash flow.

A few other process steps cost relatively little but have a huge positive impact. First, know that when you are giving credit to someone who is not in the Dun and Bradstreet database, it does not mean they won't pay, but understand you are now financing their operations. While start-ups will argue they need every customer to get the business going, like the restaurant, if your bills need to get paid before you get paid by your customers, you will run a negative cash flow forever. That is not the mark of a real business. Sure, you can get financing from the bank, with an interest rate, but then why are you financing your customer for free?

Second, your AR or credit team should reach out to your customers' accounts payable (AP) departments within a few days of billing. It helps to have established a relationship with somebody at that office, who will give your bill special attention.

Third, some customers' systems and processes are as bad as or worse than your own, so you need to make sure the invoice you send contains all the proper information for payment to go smoothly. Some companies require purchase orders in order to pay, others require you to input the invoice information directly into their systems, and still others may require you to provide proper tax information and such. Whatever excuse your customer might use not to pay you is better discovered early and corrected before the invoice is due.

Finally, not only does your AR team need to get to know the people who pay the bills for your customers, it also needs to make sure they feel important and appreciated. You need your customers' AP team working for you, not against you. Often the people paying customer bills are underpaid and underappreciated, so they will welcome any attention you give them.

While I was at Pandora, most of our customers' payment centers were in New York. To establish positive working relationships with them, we took two steps.

First, we located our AR team in the same time zone as our customers' payment centers, reducing any reasons a customer may have for missing a phone call and making person-to-person visits easier.

Second—and I learned this from our finance manager, Dennis, who headed Pandora's East Coast admin team—have your customers' accounts payable teams feel the love of your company. Every Monday or Tuesday, Dennis had his folks reach out and meet their accounts payable counterparts, bringing coffee and donuts for them. Again, just about no one pays attention to the person paying the bills, so doing that will help get you paid. As a result, Pandora's DSO dropped by more than 50 percent, and the mix of late payments declined dramatically. At the end of the day, relationships matter at all levels. So for the people you have in this function, relationship-building should be a critical part of their skill set.

7. Manage for Momentum

You need to build a solid finance team that will get you there. This means assessing who is doing the most to get the team going quickly and who is working to maintain that momentum. Staying on top of operations data and delivering it in a timely way to the management is the most important job of the finance team. You cannot run a business if you do not know where you are headed, and you cannot resource your business properly unless you know that it is growing faster than you thought or shrinking even a little.

That's why I cannot emphasize enough how much the finance team needs people who truly understand accounting, because of the level of detail required under GAAP rules to forecast depreciation, amortize costs, establish rules for capitalizing product development, and more. Those team members will also need to be detail oriented, as the forecast models have to be at the employee level, and yet have a good understanding of the data sources in the company to get the three views of data in order to make a reliable forecast.

For example, one view might be a forecast that looks at sales capacity to determine if there are enough sales reps to achieve the expected outcome. A second data point might be ensuring there are enough leads and opportunities in the pipeline to achieve the desired sales goal. The third point might be looking at history and the seasonal trends and timing for deals in order to predict the numbers for the quarter.

The finance team also needs to have some business savvy members, because it will often be the point of contact for your various functions into accounting and finance. In that role it may be asked to provide input into how best to run another department financially.

As part of your assessment, the most critical people will be those who can carry out the ongoing changes and improvements of the business processes. Because the operating numbers flow through them, they will often be the first to identify issues emerging across the company.

ASSESS THE FLOW OF INFORMATION

The next big area to assess is the current state of the company's information systems and what it will cost to bring those systems up to public-company grade to adequately run the business through the coming four to six years of growth and expansion.

This long-term horizon is important because most systems in current use by the company may not be able to scale to the growth you will likely experience. Ironically, most companies consider themselves to be data driven, yet they lack the systems to collect data quickly enough to help facilitate timely business decisions.

In almost every company I have joined to help grow the business and go public, the second biggest spend in time and money is on system upgrades and implementation. The only exception was Salesforce. When I joined Salesforce at $20 million in revenue and sixty-five employees, we were already using Oracle financials (almost unheard of for a company that size), Salesforce CRM software, of course, and ADP payroll. These systems helped us grow to more than $1 billion in revenue and over four thousand employees worldwide before we needed to upgrade. That allowed us to devote our resources to more important investments.

Why does a company need to invest so much in system upgrades and implementation? Systems not only provide the data you need to run a business; they can shrink the cycle time of any process and reduce the error rate.

By the way, an Excel spreadsheet managed by a single person is not a system. It is a slow-paced process fraught with errors, and while it may appear inexpensive, it most certainly is not, given the long-term costs that result from inaccurate and untimely operating data.

Another misconception is that systems are expensive. Of course they cost money, but installation and associated costs can be spread over three to five years. The cost of implementation will never be cheaper than at this early stage. In today's cloud environment, the cost of systems is historically low, and if you start with a base system that can last four to six years while the company grows, the costs are far outweighed by the benefits they provide. Also, as you enter year four of your existing systems, it is time to start on your final system implementation. By then you will have some idea of your potential scale, so you should begin installing your next set of enterprise resource planning (ERP) systems, which will carry you through multiple billions in revenue and last for the next decade or two.

Moreover, while you may think you are saving money by delaying the next systems upgrade, the reality is that it gets more expensive and takes longer the bigger the company gets. That is why cloud computing, even after almost fifteen years, has a huge upside as the bigger, more complex systems move to the cloud.

In preparing to go public, you must share the current and future state of your systems with other C-level management and the board. Regardless of when you start new systems implementations, they will require a behavioral change in your company.

For example, I have yet to join a company in which travel and expense (T&E) reports aren't submitted via an Excel spreadsheet with a stack of receipts. At that point, some poor accounts payable person is left to sort out how to account for the charges, which department to charge, and who if anyone approved the expenses. By the way, these expense reports inevitably are 90 to 120 days old, and yet the submitter wants to be paid the next day.

If this sounds familiar, your company already has systems issues—which will mean spending money on systems and changing your employees' behavior. This is your test case. Of course, you cannot book expenses 90 or 120 days late. Your first instinct may be to do an accrual to estimate monthly expenses. But, since no one has any idea what employees are spending, the notion of an accurate accrual is a myth.

Proper controls suggest somebody higher in the organization should agree which T&E charges are appropriate and allowable. At one company I joined we found people buying furniture for their apartments, purchasing materials for home improvements, and taking extravagant holidays around their business trips—all while billing the company. In one case a sales executive in Europe bought a Porsche on his company credit card and charged it to airfare. It sounds crazy, but it's happened. Whether you are a private or public company, you need to get your hands around these costs.

Reviewing T&E expenses is also a good way to get a handle on the moral values of your company. How many and what type of personal charges do the founders and C-level executives run through the company's T&E fund? How many folks have personal package deliveries made to the office? I know start-ups are famous for providing employee perks, but why wouldn't you have a package delivered to your home, instead of forcing the company to spend the money to receive and house your stuff?

The only way to solve these habits is to break them. That will take a change in behavior, usually backed by some straightforward and well-publicized punishment. Your employees need to realize that this is a place of work and not a package delivery drop-off point, or a purchasing agent for personal items. Yes, I have heard all of the excuses—but really, what are you spending money on that does not add value to your company? What will you do to find out the truth? T&E offers a clear example of the ways in which investing in systems ultimately saves you money.

ASSESS YOUR COMPANY CULTURE

The next area to assess is company culture, including the management styles of your founders and leadership team.

You have some questions to ask, such as: Does the executive team have the ability and desire to evolve over time? A start-up, by definition, has to grow to be successful. If that is the premise, then the management team also needs to grow, change, and bring in new management and leadership talent. This growth comes in two forms:

1. *The capacity of the existing team and founder for listening*

Are they curious about what they don't know and willing to learn from others? Reading books and reviewing Wikipedia are a good beginning, but there's a lot that can be learned only from experience—the stuff where theory meets messy, real-life challenges. Yogi Berra said it best: "In theory there is no difference between theory and practice. In practice there is." The ability of the current management team and founders to adapt to reality is critical.

2. *The ability of the existing team and founders to integrate newcomers*

At Salesforce, the team was composed of either veterans from an existing public company or people who at least had experienced public company life sometime in their careers. All of them knew, for the business to be successful, processes, systems, and employee behavior would need to change. Better yet, the start-up team appreciated that these types of changes signaled that the company was on a path to success.

It wasn't always easy. I remember posting a twenty-four-hour security service at the data center door to reinforce the fact that we needed to control our data center access or we would never pass the newly required SOX controls testing. With humor, and regular reminders to company employees, it worked. Things changed.

Later I discovered that, in fact, the Salesforce employees had always complied with the data center access rules. Instead, it was the building maintenance crew who consistently broke the rules because they regularly had to access a service panel in the same room. The armed guards helped make this discovery, and in response our controls were changed to ensure the maintenance folks were escorted in and out when they needed to be in that space. We probably never would have solved the problem of data access controls otherwise; it brought to life the importance of the controls and how practices needed to change.

Pandora was a team that had been together nearly seven years when I joined. By that point, they were as much a family as a team. Because they had become so hermetic, with so many common experiences, bringing others into the team proved a heavy challenge, to the company's detriment, I think. Fresh eyes on the business, with the understanding one has to continue to invent to grow the business, are always valuable. While a tight-knit team might have a great deal of value in terms of experience and cohesiveness, it is also likely to leave numerous opportunities for success on the table simply because it doesn't see them.

By comparison, with Yext, the founding team (who had mostly been together since high school) fully embraced new executive hires. One thing the founders did was listen well, explain what they had been doing to get to the company's current state, and try to understand what needed to be changed. As a result, the management team that has grown at Yext is a mix of those with experience and those gaining experience. Everyone has one critical focus: make the business successful.

The Yext team has learned to do that. Embedded in its culture is the strongly held belief that each employee, each executive will succeed if Yext is successful. While this may seem self-evident, the politics of many companies often lead to individuals trying to achieve success even at the expense of the company. While I will admit this was not an assessment I did previously, my experience at Yext has placed this item on my list of assessment areas.

The lesson for you is this: while it is valuable to build a strong and tight-knit executive team, that cohesion should never come at the expense of entertaining new ideas coming from outside the team.

Reinforcing this openness almost always needs to come from the top down, especially from the CEO.

DO YOUR HOMEWORK

Finally, your assessment needs to include just plain due diligence.

1. Internal Assessment

Make sure you understand your company's real issues, and make sure the team is working on or willing to address such issues.

- Are there any pending lawsuits?
- Are there any employee complaints? (Visit Glassdoor.com to get a sense of this.)
- Are there any concerns from existing customers? (Look at Yelp or any other review-driven site.)
- Where do you rate in customer and employee satisfaction?

You need to make management and the board aware of these assessments and help develop a strategy for dealing with any challenges.

2. Auditors

Reach out to the company's auditors. In speaking with them, it is critical to understand if they have been performing audits for public companies or only private ones. Private company audits typically don't work with as much detail as is required for a public company, so your company's prior quarters may need additional review under public company guidelines. You may need to replace your auditors with a public company auditor who can determine what it will take to make your company SOX compliant.

By the way, this is the point when you should be hard at work obtaining that compliance, as fixing any roadblocks to the Fed's approval can sometimes take a year or more. The most common pain point usually deals with system controls, in particular with having adequate controls over software or product changes and limited end-user access to the system to make any data changes without third-party review and approval. More on this in chapter 9.

Note that it is rare that a material weakness or significant deficiency will have an impact on the company with respect to valuation, unless of course it forces the filing of a financial restatement. If this happens you have much bigger issues.

3. Legal Counsel

In conversations with the company's outside legal counsel, you should try to get a sense of the following:

- The type of commercial contracts the company engages in
- Any favorable or unfavorable terms the company may get going forward (better to know them now than to get surprised later)
- The state of the stock records the law firm keeps for their early-stage company clients
- Any extraordinary arrangements regarding issue of stock warrants or other terms around share granting
- An understanding of the culture of the firm, specifically regarding any possible harassment issues or circumstances that will create issues in the future
- Any sudden terminations or other actions regarding employees

Ultimately, the goal of the assessment phase is to get as complete a picture as possible of the company and the supporting professionals you will depend upon as you start down the path to your IPO. Identify as early as possible those weaknesses and systemic problems that will need to be addressed over the subsequent eighteen to twenty-four months.

CHAPTER 4

THE PEOPLE

With this chapter we start to build for the IPO. The process of IPO readiness takes two things to get underway:

1. The right team of people
2. The right systems

We will discuss what to look for and how to approach the decisions you have to make at this stage. Keep in mind that, though the systems are critical, you need the right people to make the proper decisions on how those systems should be set up.

So first, the team.

Hiring the proper management team starts with an assessment of the existing executive and founding teams' strengths and weaknesses. Is the executive team oriented to sales or marketing or product development? Does anyone on the team care about customer success? (All executives should; however, most do not.) Some executive teams are product-centric; for them it's all about the technology. While this is a necessary element, and even an advantage in a company's early years, it is not sufficient for a successful long-term business. You have to have

a management team that can describe the product's value to the customer today as well as the long-term vision of the solution and product
offerings for the future. Does your team have that capability, or will
you need to hire for it?

Hiring to bolster the team's weaknesses is critical to ensure all
areas of the business are covered. Leave some area uncovered, and it
will show up in lower valuations for the business going forward, as the
team will not operate effectively or efficiently while trying to cover a
shortfall in a function or the functional leader.

The best example I know of this was at Salesforce. In the early
days, we faced a strong technical competitor. Their solution had more
features, was mostly cloud computing, and was advanced in terms of
offerings and pricing. Unfortunately for them (and fortunately for us),
the competitor's management team was quite technically focused,
so its presentations and meetings were all about the technology. The
presenters were engineers, and they consistently failed to capture the
imagination of the audience or customer. The company advertised in
airports and used traditional software marketing methods to describe
and measure their company. In other words, there was no energy in
the vision.

Meanwhile, at Salesforce, while our offering had slightly fewer features, our potential customers could feel the vision and energy in our
user-oriented presentations. In the early days of Salesforce, you could
see the now famous "no software" logo and the underpinnings of SaaS
described as "utility computing." Of course, we had the not-so-secret
weapons of our charismatic founders, Marc Benioff and Parker Harris.
Marc naturally commanded an audience and painted a great vision
with relatable analogies. Potential customers didn't always buy into our
story, but at least they understood the business direction and the path
we were on. Couple that with Parker's ability to describe our technology and our product development strategy, and we had an unbeatable
combination. We ran no advertising, only word-of-mouth marketing, customer events, and executive gatherings, all driving home our
no-software campaign. It was clearly a radical vision, but we backed it
up with execution.

The goals of this marketing effort were to attract not just prospective customers but also prospective talent.

In building a start-up into a $17 billion company, on its way to $40 billion, you need to recruit several successive classes of employees. The first generation, in the early days, was passionate and committed to the notion that they could build—or at least lay the foundation for—all the functions of the business. These folks would do anything, at any time, to get stuff done. This stuff was not just mundane technology such as package software or processes, but innovative solutions to building product, marketing the product, and making the customer successful, all while executing in the most efficient manner. These early employees were builders; all they needed to know was where the company was going, and they took it from there.

Typically, employees at this early stage in a company's story have some unique traits, notably a need to be risk-takers and heroes. But they also are often inexperienced. It is rare to find experienced individuals who are the kind of risk-takers start-ups need, but risk-taking and breaking the rules are key attributes in hiring.

Early stage companies usually attract youthful talent because they have nothing to lose and they see a huge upside; hence many hires come right out of school. They are smart people, but too often they're simply inexperienced. Successful start-up early hires need to know when breaking the rules is a benefit and when doing what has already been done is efficient. At Salesforce, utility computing broke the rules for software delivery and ease of use for customers. However, doing business with contracts and requiring purchase orders from large customers was a necessary condition—here, breaking the rules was of no value to the business.

Thus, in hiring you need to sort out those candidates who are not only looking for a mission to join but who also already have the specific skills, or are quick learners, to help the company succeed. The right combination of experience and thinking differently adds value to a business. Let's see how this comes into play in specific departments.

ENGINEERING AND PRODUCT DEVELOPMENT

Hiring rule breakers is especially important in engineering and product development. That's because the engineering team needs to be consistently providing innovative solutions and to be cognizant of the changing competitive and developmental technology environment.

We see these developments all the time—the dial-up environment moving to the Internet, the Internet moving to 4G and 5G technology, on-premise computing moving to cloud computing, and, of course, user interfaces such as browsers moving to mobile search to voice search to artificial intelligence, and, in the foreseeable future, to quantum computing. In each of these shifts, the companies that couldn't adapt to the new competitive and technology world ultimately died. According to Moore's Law, which states that computing power doubles every two years, these shifts are coming ever faster.

In short, you need to hire engineers who can master these changing environments in order to maintain the company's competitive advantage and to ensure its product lines keep their freshness. Typically you find this quality in talented engineers fresh from school, because they are not burdened by the old rules and approaches to solutions. Many companies become so burdened by past architectures that their tardy attempts to keep up cause them to slip behind and, as a result, allow starts-up to enter the picture with a fresh vision and more contemporary view of the world. Examples of once-mighty companies that hung on to the status quo too long are numerous: Blackberry, Nokia, Yellow Cabs, Seibel Systems, Barnes and Noble, Sears, and on and on.

By comparison to the endless search for youthful innovation in engineering and product development, in sales, marketing, and finance you need youthful energy and ambition, sure, but you also need individuals who have a lot of experience. In these areas, experience counts more than rule breaking. In sales, marketing, and finance, establishing known, successful processes can facilitate rapid growth.

Why? Let's look at each department.

SALES

It is great to have young, hard-charging individuals on the sales team. Every company, no matter what its size, needs this type of sales talent to sustain itself over the long term. That said, generating sales also requires two more things: a structured process and a strong training program.

These structured processes vary greatly with the company. The sales playbook at Salesforce was very different from the one at Yext. At first glance they seemed similar in style, but a more detailed look showed their very different philosophies and executions. Every business has its own sales playbook, and that means you need experienced sales veterans who know how to develop your company's unique version.

Preparing that playbook is only the beginning. You also need to train employees in your unique sales philosophies and practices and to put into place an infrastructure to enable the playbook and the process it demands. So that means you also need to find an experienced trainer who has done this before, who has put together a successful sales training process in the past. The goal of this trainer should be to ensure that all company salespeople understand how the company approaches a customer, provides that customer the best solution, and establishes the basis for a long-term relationship.

When a start-up has yet to achieve market recognition and is offering innovative solutions to customer problems, it's the relationship between the sales executive and the customer that closes the deal. Too often the hiring of hardworking sellers misses this key point: your sales executives need to know how to build trust. While some companies focus on hiring a young and hungry sales team, this tactic can backfire. An inexperienced, callow, or shallow salesperson, no matter how smart and energetic, won't be able to build the trusting relationships you need.

Speaking of trusting relationships, in every successful company there comes a moment when it is imperative to place sellers in different cities. Many companies attempt to run a central office and fly their sellers to other cities for customer calls. Over the long haul, this doesn't work out. Not only do you run up travel expenses, but location matters. Like-minded potential customers talk to each other. They look for connections to others in their area, and they look for validation of products and services being sold. Flying in and out does not cultivate that kind of buzz. Not to mention that, like it or not, cultures, interests, events, activities, and values vary between all of the big markets.

A seller who does not appreciate, understand, exhibit, or participate in local culture has a disadvantage when it comes to establishing trust and credibility. Try sending a New York seller to Dallas during football season and see what happens.

I saw a classic example of the difference between local sales teams versus drop-ins at a California company I worked for with an accounts receivable collection problem. It seemed odd to me that 60 percent of the company's business happened east of the Mississippi, yet our collections and customer service departments were on the West Coast. The time zone differences alone caused undue harm to our customer relationships and cycle times.

Happily, we placed collections teams in Chicago and New York, which increased productivity by more than 30 percent and reduced DSOs of receivables to less than fifty days. The lesson is that bottom-line personal relationships do matter, whether you are in sales, customer service, or accounts receivable collections. Being in the same time zone, with shared cultures, values, and interests, will have a positive influence on your profitability.

That said, take care when placing sales teams in new regions. Invariably when taking this step, companies send one of their better sellers to a new location, moving him or her from, say, San Francisco to Chicago. That's what we did at Salesforce. Until we noticed what happens when you transfer a wildly successful salesperson to a new territory: complete failure. Why? Because this seller, who had built numerous trusting relationships in San Francisco, had no such relationships in Chicago and no time to develop them. Rather than removing top talent from the milieu where they are most productive, we learned to hire the best talent we could find already established in the new location.

MARKETING

Here, again, youthful energy is needed and can accomplish a lot, but it is insufficient to get you where you want to be. Marketing is complex, so first you need to determine what type of marketing you want to do, and then you need to hire experienced talent that knows how to do that kind of work. Once you have that team in place, you can supplement with new talent that can be trained over time.

In my experience, marketing must accomplish three crucial things:

- Lead generation
- Customer awareness
- Brand building: company and product positioning

Over time your business will need to cover all three aspects of marketing. Understanding the stage you are in will inform the type of people you need to hire. Let's look at each.

1. Lead Generation

Lead generation is ongoing and permanent. After all, that is how you feed your sales organization. So a person who is process oriented, yet savvy about demographics, customer spending patterns, and the use of the Internet, is critical right from the start. In all the companies that I have been involved with, this initial lead generation hire is one of the most critical. It also has been the most difficult. It requires a blend of skillful mastery of web presence (such as white papers, webinars, and key word searches) and of capturing inbound prospects that visit your company website. (This, most often, seems to be overlooked in start-ups.)

Yet lead generation also demands mastery of such old-fashioned techniques as buying mailing lists in sales territories, using demographics to profile prospective customers, and creating targeted messaging marketing campaigns based on that profiling.

Finally, your prospective lead generator needs to exercise these skills while simultaneously and quickly learning your business, vision, and customers. As difficult as this person may be to find, this job is so critical to the company that you should spend all the time you need looking for the best fit. Once you do, you should keep looking for someone even better.

2. Customer Awareness

Once you have the lead generation job covered, it is time to start the search for a customer awareness expert. That means you are looking for someone to raise awareness and begin to position the company in the minds of customers and prospects.

Awareness building can be fun, but it also requires a skilled networker who thinks differently about getting your company noticed. Salesforce had a number of such people. Precisely because this team thinks outside the box, you will have to get used to their seemingly crazy ideas, such as renting out AT&T Park for friends and family to wander through the infield and outfield, sit in the dugouts, and hit balls from the batting cage. When the customer awareness team at Salesforce suggested this idea, it sounded like fun, but we were also just a $30 million business, and burning cash. As the CFO who had just joined the company, and who had never done anything like this, I wondered if my new employer was out of its mind. But we went ahead and did it. Amazingly, the press coverage we received—and more importantly, the word-of-mouth marketing we enjoyed—proved well worth it.

A more traditional awareness-raising program at Salesforce took the form of customer events where we showed off new products, or where people could meet the management team and ask questions. The key to these types of smaller events, best described in *Behind the Cloud* by Marc Benioff, was their open invitation to customers, prospects, press, and investors. They were effective precisely because they brought these key groups together in one informal setting: lunches, usually at well-known restaurants in the local city, where they could ask each other questions. More importantly, each session featured a formal Q&A, so challenging questions could be asked, and everyone heard the same answer. The event wasn't scripted; it was real. It moved the needle on our marketing and awareness.

3. Brand Building: Company and Product Positioning

Awareness-generating experiences contribute to a company's understanding of itself, its markets, and its customers. This understanding becomes the basis for the company's creation of its brand. Managing that creation—and then maintaining and growing it—is also a unique skill, and typically it requires a different type of marketing talent. This marketing leadership must use images and selected words and know where to message the company solutions, be it TV, social media, web search, and so forth.

The key to all of this is change, adaptation, and evolution. You need to maintain a constant assessment of your company awareness in the market, positioning, and brand building. Your marketing department must evolve with your business as it grows and brings on new product lines, moves to adjacent markets, and expands internationally. The marketing department's task is to communicate these changes to the marketplace in a consistent manner with a timely and well-thought-out approach.

Searching for an executive to manage the department through these changes—someone who has more than one approach to these issues—is critical and difficult. Think of it this way: your marketing department is like a rock band. You are looking for a band with longevity, that can change its style as quickly as popular music tastes change, and still play in top form. What you don't want is a one-hit wonder, no matter how talented the band is. There are numerous books on this topic, which you should search out to help understand how to build a brand, and what type of leader you need to do this successfully. My favorites include *The Tipping Point* by Malcolm Gladwell (2000, Little, Brown and Company) and *Get to Aha!* by Andy Cunningham (2017, McGraw-Hill Education).

FINANCE

As you look toward an IPO, you likely will need to rebuild your finance team from the ground up. I divide finance team members into four types: hoarders, finders, builders, and maintainers. Let's look at who you have now and who you will need when preparing to go public.

1. Hoarders

In a start-up, the finance team typically has been hired to focus on simple bookkeeping, working with either Excel spreadsheets or QuickBooks. But in the world of public corporations, that's not enough. In all my years helping companies go public, I have found only one start-up finance person who could handle the transition to a public company.

Unfortunately, and too often, rebuilding your finance team is not a simple matter of replacing old employees (who usually enjoy founders' stock) with new ones. Certain complications are likely to arise. At first, many of the old guard will try to protect their jobs by sequestering information, by resisting changes in the process and organization, and by misrepresenting their roles and responsibilities. I call these folks hoarders. They operate under the misconception that if they alone hold the keys to certain information, they'll be considered indispensable to the company, and, therefore, will not lose their jobs.

Nothing could be further from the truth. In a growing company, everything must change continuously. Hoarders, by their behavior, inhibit this change, and in doing so, they damage the company's health. The hoarders must be transitioned out politely but quickly, as you bring in what I call the finders.

2. Finders and Builders

The finders make up your new first team. Their task is to sort out the past and set the stage for the future. They need to learn how things have been done—and fast—so they can help reorient processes toward the company's future needs. The challenge with the finders is they often don't have the requisite experience in how to build this first generation of processes, tools, and systems.

That's why you need a second team: the builders.

In the early stages of readying the company for an IPO, one needs a combination of finders and builders. The finders understand what is; the builders have to put in place what is going to be. When you are getting into go mode for your IPO, you need to sort out the type of person you are looking for in each category.

Finders are detail oriented. They can reconcile even the messiest accounts. They can identify details and create backup for transactions. They are great on spreadsheets, but probably not exposed to ERP systems or other tools. In many cases, finders may not understand the business entirely, but they are invaluable in knowing how the business is getting done. For finders, important hiring criteria include previous work accomplishments and a strong work ethic. Some finders can be schooled to become builders, but they are the exception, not the rule.

By comparison, builders are the people who develop that first process or implement the first system for the company. They create the tools by which the company can operate and scale over time.

While hiring finders can be challenging, hiring builders is even harder. Builders need to share the company vision and the vision of a finance infrastructure that will get the company to $1 billion in revenues, then $3 billion in revenues, then $5 billion and beyond. A top-notch builder needs good technical skills, good process skills, excellent problem-solving skills, and even better communication skills.

At industry conferences, when I talk about taking a company public, I often say my biggest regret is that I didn't study psychology along with accounting. As a finance leader, my perpetual challenge has been getting people to solve problems and change their behavior in the best interest of the company.

So when I am interviewing for builders, I look not only for basic breadth of knowledge, technical skills, and demonstrated problem-solving skills, but for great interpersonal skills. I want to hire a person who gets along well with others. Start-ups are stressful enough, and that stress continues well beyond IPO day, so nice people are important. Look for builders who possess all the necessary skills, and who also have fun building.

Note also, once you hire your builders, you'll need to manage them to grow their careers internally. They will be critical to developing future management, and as you cross $1 billion in revenue, they will need to build the processes and systems again to get to $5 billion and beyond.

3. Maintainers

As your builders learn the processes and find the appropriate systems to use, keep in mind you are rotating out the finders and starting to put in some of the third type of finance professional: maintainers—the folks who run and execute what has been built and can improve on the current process. Maintainers have experience in larger companies, process-improvement skills, and highly specialized skills in various areas of the business. You should hire maintainers based somewhat on the specific systems you use, because they bring valuable experience in those systems along with them, thus reducing transition time.

Interestingly, both Yext and Salesforce recruited early, large-company executives to take the risk and help them grow. At Salesforce, Jim Steele and I joined at about the same time. Jim came from IBM and Ariba; I came from Autodesk and HP. The big risk for a start-up company betting on large-company executives is that most $1 billion-plus companies are filled not with builders but with maintainers. Luckily, Jim and I did bring some builder experience, and though we took some time adjusting to small company practices (like having to schedule our own appointments and traveling coach class), those companies survived our arrival.

LEGAL

Speaking as a finance person, I can tell you a talented general counsel (GC) can be a great partner, helping lead the way through the SEC filings. So find someone who has SEC knowledge, understands contract law, is an excellent negotiator, has a sense of humor, and possesses great business sense. (Most legal decisions come down to trade-offs of risk and business needs, rarely legal trade-offs.) I have partnered with some great GCs in my time. I still keep track of them. They are always the first people I go to when I have a new IPO opportunity.

OTHERS CRITICAL HIRES

There are other critical hires when ramping up to an IPO. They include an experienced chief accounting officer (CAO), a controller, and a planning and forecasting leader. In addition to a good sense of business, all these team leaders must have experience leading teams and hiring people. When I hire these folks, I ask who they have worked with that they would plan to hire into their teams. A network of talented people will jump-start the team, getting solutions and processes put in place quickly. If your leaders already know how to recruit their teams, then you are on your way to a successful start-up.

A NOTE ON RECRUITING

As a company grows, it will require different skills and experience from all its employees, so it should not be surprising that a company will experience turnover at all levels. It is a rare start-up that attracts its top talent—except perhaps in engineering—from the get-go. For example, many start-up companies find a different CFO to take them public. They also tend to change sales leadership in the $300 million to $500 million revenue range, usually because they did not have a sales leader who could scale to such large numbers.

As CFO, I personally get involved in all hires until leaders in each department can demonstrate that we all have the same values and goals. Needless to say, you are going to make hiring mistakes—I have, and I will continue to do so. But you can mitigate the damage of a bad hire by continually recruiting, continually looking for that better person either inside or outside the company. If your business is always growing, you are always hiring.

Further, sales recruiting is different from hiring engineers or financial people. So you need recruiting specialists in all three areas, and in each, the recruiting process needs to become a machine, one that works from a clear profile of the recruits you are looking for. For a salesperson, it is how many sales clubs they made during their time at previous employers; for an engineer, it is how many patent developments they were involved in; for a finance person, it is the processes and systems they changed and the result of that implementation. I see too many recruiting agencies default to LinkedIn and throw resumes at a hiring manager with no purpose other than to get people hired regardless of their fit. A manager who hasn't characterized the kind of employee the company is looking for ends up more confused than productive.

COMPANY CULTURE

Malcolm Gladwell's *Outliers* (2008, Little, Brown and Company) contends that individual and, ultimately, company success is not powered by the smartest, hardest-driven, or most experienced people, but rather by the system the company establishes in terms of decision-making, project cycle times, performance expectations, communication channels, and a myriad of other factors. That means when hiring, you need to give priority to those people who will fit your company's culture.

This understanding will also help you think about letting people go. In my own career, the hiring mistakes I made were often because I hired a candidate for his or her skill set, not based on how the person was going to fit our system. Rather than thinking of letting people go—even people with superb resumes—as cruel, think of how it can be beneficial to them. You're enabling them to find the company whose culture fits their personality and style. Replacing them with someone who may not be quite as talented, but who is a good fit, can be equally beneficial.

When you're leading your company's charge toward an IPO, your active participation in the hiring process is important. Meeting candidates and discussing the pros and cons of candidates with your hiring managers helps everyone level-set which types of hires the company wants. At minimum, you want folks who willingly share data, ideas, and experience (that is, no hoarders), and of course, they need to fit the personality of the company and its culture.

As you build a team, you also need to encourage new people to think differently about their roles and their contributions to the company. New hires need to be able to adapt best practices they've learned elsewhere to your company culture. If I had brought the famous HP

Way to Salesforce, it could have killed the company or at least I would have failed and been fired. Salesforce had its own way. For example, we often had a world-class yoga instructor accompany us to our offsites. Rather than take a coffee break, we took thirty-minute yoga breaks. Like hot tubs and avocado toast, this practice was very Northern California. It fit with the Salesforce culture, so it wasn't intrusive. In fact, the yoga breaks actually made us more productive. Would I attempt this practice at, say, IBM, with its very different culture? No, because it's not a match for IBM.

The message is this: first, understand your company's culture, then determine the skills you are going to need to get to the IPO and beyond, and then start recruiting.

CHAPTER 5

THE SYSTEMS

While picking the team to take your company public is critical, choosing the corporate information management system to support that team is a crucial decision, and one that will have lasting implications for your company.

In the panel discussions and meetings I have had with CFOs and VCs, the decision to put systems in sooner rather than later is controversial.

On the one hand, you don't want to spend the money to put in systems if you have not yet proven the business model or identified a significant market opportunity. On the other hand, if you don't put in those systems early enough you won't have the data you need to make it a successful business. So what should you do? For me, the answer is that the least expensive and most productive time to install business systems is when you are relatively small and have formulated a long-term vision of the future.

Salesforce is the only company I have been with that had adopted a formal set of business systems early on. At $20 million in revenue, we already were using a version of Oracle ERP. Obviously, this system did not feature all of the available bells and whistles, but at least we had an

ERP system to capture our basic product and financial data. In time, we added billing and other systems that facilitated employee resources and established a simple data warehouse.

This early adoption is not typical, though. Many young companies begin using QuickBooks, but that simply doesn't qualify as a system for a growing business, mostly due to the lack of controls around data and access—a standard for meeting the requirements of Sarbanes-Oxley. You need to start with a system that will grow in sophistication as you do.

HOW TO CHOOSE A SYSTEM

To choose the right systems for your company, you need to consider several issues.

1. Suite or Best of Breed?

Do you want a single suite system that does almost everything, or should you go with best of breed in each application category?

A single suite provides better integration for a majority of the processes, but it does not provide the best system in each category. By comparison, best of breed allows you to select the best provider in each system category, but you may give something up when it comes to integration. NetSuite, for example, offers a great small and midsize company general ledger (GL) and basic ERP. However, its CRM solution simply cannot keep up with Salesforce and its ever-expanding features and functionality.

Are you willing to suboptimize on one process versus another? What is the impact of such a decision? There have been numerous debates and opinions about the best approach. Ultimately your decision rests with the scale of the business you hope to achieve and your ability to manage more than one vendor.

2. Multi-Tenant

The cost of a solution depends on the size of your initial deployment of that solution and the appropriateness of the solution to your needs. Make sure, however, you are selecting a cloud solution that is truly multi-tenant. A number of providers will tell you they are "cloud" because you access them via the Internet. That should only be the beginning. Multi-tenant means that the provider's customers are using the same computers and access that you do, not just a faux front end. Salesforce is the classic example of multi-tenant.

3. Application Programming Interface (API)

Another important question concerns the potential provider's API. The number of standard APIs your provider has compared to other cloud vendors determines how much flexibility you have to integrate your cloud solutions. Zendesk is a great example of a service ticketing company that provides a great number of APIs to other cloud vendors. Salesforce as well has a strong API catalog. APIs are critical for integrating your solutions and adding productivity to your solutions.

4. Cloud or On-Premises?

Cloud. Definitely. Why? Because in my experience, on-premises solutions can become so expensive and so fraught with hidden costs that it becomes increasingly difficult to keep up with customer requests for process changes and new software releases. That in turn can force a company to invest in its own IT department and then hire and train folks on how to customize and modify the in-house solution.

Once customization happens, upgrades become nearly impossible, and support costs skyrocket. New features and functions fail to make it into operations due to the hazard an upgrade presents. In short: a young company doesn't want to deal with any of this when it is trying to conserve capital and focus on growth.

By comparison, cloud solutions typically deliver upgrades and enhancements two or more times a year. But a word of warning: resist the temptation to customize a cloud solution to fit your process. If you start customizing, you will lose the benefits of any new features, as well as the ability to upgrade. Instead, change your processes to fit the solution you have selected and stay current on your provider's regularly provided solutions. My rule of thumb is to remain one version behind the current release. I don't even buy a new smartphone until it has been on the market six months. Why? Because new technology—and especially software—always has bugs. So let other customers find and fix those bugs before you upgrade.

Once you have made your choices, commit yourself to fully understanding the solution you have selected. You must know your systems inside out to take full advantage of them, especially to help you define your future processes and upgrades.

Again, if you start to customize because you have convinced yourself you are smarter or your problems are unique, you will lose the value of the cloud solution. Returning to current releases will cost you significantly more money—not just on IT, but worse, in a loss of productivity in the functions your system is supporting.

That's why it's almost always better to spend your money not on hiring more programmers but instead on hiring more qualified system administrators who can make the basic cloud solution work via the tools provided by the vendor. We'll talk more about that next.

HOW TO HIRE SYSTEM ADMINISTRATORS

Of course, once you have chosen your systems, you're going to need qualified system administrators who can get the most out of those systems for your company. In addition, you'll need a data control specialist to manage data element definitions and resolve or control the uses of those definitions. Finally, you'll need folks who are experts at API integrations, who can update them and stay abreast of the latest in API technology.

How do you find these people?

One way to hire great people for these tasks is to determine, before you hire them, what systems they've used in the past. You'll find most have a lot of experience in old, on-premises systems. Knowing you will have to train and educate them on cloud solutions is critical information when planning a new system implementation.

For example, in sales I would generally not hire a sales rep who was inexperienced using Salesforce. It is a widely used CRM solution, has best practices, and is very powerful. If you hire a sales rep with no experience using Salesforce, you will have to incur additional training costs for that hire. Otherwise, the inexperienced rep will likely not understand the importance of data capture and the details behind keeping customer information correct and current.

For finance employees, I like to know if they have used Salesforce (because so much information is available there) and then either FinancialForce, NetSuite, or Workday. All of these systems are set up on relational data warehouses and, thus, are much more capable than the transactional systems of old. Data collection, usage, and reporting also are much stronger, but how they work in terms of relational data structures versus aggregating the sum of transactions takes a different mindset. It is critical that your finance team can work in a relational data structure architectural universe.

For system administrators, you are looking for people who are experienced users of the specific system; you want them to have knowledge of the APIs the system can use and the data elements of the particular solutions you chose to run the company. In this role, experience counts, along with hard examples of process improvements.

THE CORE SYSTEMS

You'll need several core systems in place to prepare your company to go public.

1. General Ledger (GL)

First, you need a GL that contains the chart of accounts and becomes your system of record for audits and Sarbanes-Oxley controls. There are a number of systems available, from big to small. To decide which one is the best fit for you, determine the expected size of your company five years from now and use that number to guide your choice.

Keep in mind that revenue dollars are not the only measure you need to apply, but also transaction volume and complexity. If you have a company with small-dollar/high-volume transactions, make sure you stress-test your GL selection before signing up with a provider.

Also, determine whether your business will be domestic only or whether you will have international subsidiaries, and if so, how many. There are five key questions regarding international subsidiaries:

- How does your GL system handle subsidiary consolidations?
- How much can the system do automatically versus manually intervening at key steps to complete an accurate consolidation?
- Does the system handle multiple currencies?
- How does the process of revaluing the financials happen?
- Finally, can you set up the chart of accounts and the basic reporting to deal with international statutory requirements for local country reporting?

Each of these should determine the expense and impact on your accounting process for selecting a general ledger.

The most salient question to ask when selecting a GL system is this: What does it not do compared to the other options? Knowing what it does not do will clarify either the manual effort required or the additional systems you will have to install.

2. Billing System

Your GL suite solution might be able to provide a basic billing solution, but not all GL solutions do. If they do provide a billing solution, how well does it fit your process and transaction volume? This depends upon how your company bills the customer and whether your business is usage-based, license-based, or simply product- or SKU-based.

One critical consideration in billing is transactional volume. Here, too, there are a number of questions you must address. For example, how many SKUs will be used? In other words, is your business defined by small-dollar/large-volume transactions or a limited number of large dollar transactions each month?

If you will be conducting business internationally, you must determine if your billing system can operate in multiple currencies. If so, it also must be able to provide information and accounts receivable in those currencies, and to pass foreign currency values to your GL.

At Yext, we started with a billing system that, according to the vendor, could handle foreign currency billings. But we failed to ask whether the system also carried AR balances and backlog balances in those currencies. Oops—those functions required another set of spreadsheets and manual entry.

Additionally, when considering billing systems, ask potential vendors how many APIs their billing systems have, compared to other vendors. No billing system can stand alone for long; so knowing what you can and cannot connect to will be critical to your long-term decision-making.

The more functions a billing system can handle, the more options you have between your GL system and your billing system. Whether best of breed or suite, your billing system should be capable of the following:

- Providing detailed accounts receivable information, by customer and invoice
- Providing or integrating into a quoting solution
- Carrying your product SKUs and prices
- Invoicing customers

Because your billing solution is so critical, you should use the processes the solution vendor provides to ensure that the billing solution is set up well enough to continue to be sufficient for up to five years of anticipated business operations. Because changing this type of solution is so time consuming, you don't want to have to deal with a transition any sooner. Further, start planning the swap well before that five-year mark, and keep current on the latest changes in billing solutions along the way.

How will you know it's time to change? Transaction volume fluctuations and transaction complexity typically drive the need to rebuild your billing system. Geographic diversity as well will cause a change. Even if you stay with your current vendor, other changes will come along. For instance, you will look at your business differently over time. Also, your vendor will add enhancements you are not using that you should consider implementing. Finally, and inevitably, you will need to keep your billing systems current with technology as well as congruent with the latest statutory requirements, such as sales and value-added taxes (VATs) or the unique statutory reporting requirements within a given country. Plan your way into these changes, allowing eighteen to thirty months to make the changes and get the new solutions implemented properly for the next scale of the business.

3. Human Resources Management System (HRMS)

The selection of your HRMS will depend upon many factors, some internal, others external. Let's take the internal considerations first.

Your entire workforce will interact with your HRMS, thus ease of use and an excellent and obvious workflow are critical benchmarks for this system. A user-friendly, self-service application will free your HR professionals to spend their time on real, not just data, issues.

That said, it is critical that the data be correct as it drives so many other business systems. Proper input controls and reviews help ensure the data is correct, and the system you select should provide such tools to facilitate these checks on the data. Obviously, that is true in payroll, but it also is true in travel and entertainment, cost allocation, and, of course, your benefits solutions. So much of your internal business information will come from your HRMS and related solutions.

As with your billing system, robust APIs are a necessary condition for your HRMS. This solution will need to interface with your stock compensation solution to keep track of stock grants and the always-difficult stock-compensation expense calculation.

Externally, your HRMS must meet global requirements for keeping personal information safe. Of course, privacy rules vary across countries, so this system needs to comply with different jurisdictions' regulations. Do your homework and make sure your solution can meet these varying and changing governmental requirements.

Self-service, ease of use, strong workflow for approvals, and APIs that work with your GL, payment solution, and HRMS solutions—there are a number of products that fit these needs. Find the one that meets the needs of your company. Once again, it will need to do its job for five years—and, as you approach that date, be prepared to review its performance against the changing nature of your company, regulations, and evolving technology, and replace as necessary.

These core systems—GL, billing, and HRMS—form the critical center of your data infrastructure. Your selection review should include performance benchmarks and compatibility, and you should discuss with each potential vendor the working relationships they have with the other vendors. Further, you need to find out how well these providers help with implementation and project management. I have yet to work at a company that is expert in either implementation or project management for systems like these.

BEYOND THE CORE

To round out the core system group, consider the following productivity tools. While these may seem trivial, they actually can have a better return on investment (ROI) than most of the core systems.

Here they are, in order of importance:

- A data warehouse for holding the integrated data and to conduct analysis and reporting
- A procure-to-payment system to ensure proper controls over purchases other than T&E
- A cash banking system that manages receipts, cash, and payments to optimize your cash balances
- A CRM solution to manage customer information and sales opportunities

These four systems can make a difference in productivity within your business.

1. Business Intelligence Considerations

The business intelligence (BI) needs of a company offer an opportunity not only to improve productivity but also to enforce data standards.

How many meetings have you sat through where the discussion revolved around not the business at hand but whose data was correct? Trustworthy data standards circumvent that problem and lay the foundation for the use of artificial intelligence tools going forward.

Ease of use is a critical data standard factor for non-IT users. So each function should have the capability for ad hoc reporting and tools to support searches for trends. If you repeatedly find yourself in an IT queue, then the system, no matter how powerful, has failed you. How many steps to an answer? How long to resolve errors? Too many steps, too much time—these make your IT selection user-unfriendly.

One solution is to have a few data object managers on board to ensure consistent definitions and data uses. Also, these folks become what I call the company standard report owners. That is, they ensure that the standard, agreed-upon reports can only be modified with an end user owner in agreement and the timing of the change already determined. Changing data elements before a period ends—or in the middle of a period—then losing the historical comparison can be extremely impactful to a business. Proper information technology change control becomes most important when managing a data warehouse.

2. Cash Banking Considerations

The benefits of a cash banking system should not be underrated. For example, at Yext we installed a cash banking solution between our banks and our general ledger. This solution provided information needed to facilitate bank reconciliations on the GL, set workflow limits on cash sweeps in holding accounts, and set up real-time balances for our bank accounts in the world, along with adequate controls.

Implementing this solution saved us an average of five days of reconciliation work. This proved an extraordinary advantage because, during our period of highest growth, we weren't attenuating at a pace of one day every quarter. This solution also gave us real-time balances and transaction reviews to help find errors or misdirected funds.

3. T&E and Procurement System Benefits

The T&E and procurement systems help place controls in high-volume transactions such as travel expense reports and purchases ranging from desktop computers to the soft drinks available in the office. Both are transactional and need workflow controls to pass SOX controls.

4. CRM Solution Benefits

Finally, a CRM solution is important to having a single view of your customer and to assessing important leads and opportunities. A CRM solution ensures you can measure sales activity and monitor sales success down to the sales rep level.

Determining the best systems for your needs is critical—even decisive—to success both when you are starting out and then as you grow. Make sure you have the proper, forward-thinking team in the room and arm them with a set of procedures to get to a proper solution. The cost of this process only grows with the size and complexity of your operation. So start your systems process early, when costs are lower, and then upgrade once you learn where your initial solutions will limit you and where they may no longer fulfill the business's needs.

Don't be misled: fulfilling your business's needs does not mean hiring a large number of people to move data around on spreadsheets. That solution is error-prone, late to the table with data, and difficult to share. Rather, you want easy-to-use solutions that offer timely or real-time data to provide metrics essential to running your business.

Think about your systems not merely as a cost to your business, but as tools to enable you to be more aggressive in your business operations. This new perspective will change how you think about your systems and solutions, and it will transform how you run your day-to-day business.

BIG DATA AND AI

Finally, big data and artificial intelligence have emerged as key tools in improving company performance. Both use extensive historical data to find trends, anomalies, and patterns.

Big data and AI will improve your processes, make your business quicker to react to changes, and, at the end of the day, substantially reduce your transaction cycle times. At the very least they can help you reduce audit fees and times. Why? Because audits look for patterns and anomalies—precisely what AI and big data, in particular, are best at: uncovering divergences from standards. That is true also for billing, pricing, and any other type of transactional data.

For example, billing systems should not be looking at transactions only based on prices, but also based upon customer business size, industry segment, and even time of year. Right now, that data may be useless to your decision-making, but it won't be long before it becomes relevant and important. Start your enhanced data gathering now and think of this added expense not as a drag on costs, but as an investment into the future state of your business.

Ultimately, your business transactions are data, so it follows that these powerful new data-crunching technologies can help you make faster and better business decisions.

CHAPTER 6

GOVERNANCE

Governance in business can be defined as the processes that ensure the effective and efficient use of resources enabling an organization to achieve its goals. . . . Typically there are seven elements of good governance. It is participatory, consensus oriented, accountable, transparent, responsive, effective, and efficient.

Anonymous

Arguably, governance is the most difficult issue you will face when preparing a company to operate as a public corporation.

Until this point, the company operated unfettered by outside forces other than the market and potential competitors. Now, as it institutes numerous reporting systems and controls, the company can't help but feel overwhelmed, laden with procedures, approvals, and reviews by outside parties, or stifled by surrendering its freedom of action. This feeling becomes even more profound in a founder-led company that has not yet started to diversify decision-making.

Governance is perceived as a minefield. That's why I am devoting a full chapter to prepare you for its successful implementation.

Before we begin, a reminder: whether public or private, a successful company almost always has good governance. The only additional issue with public companies is the requirement to have a third party assess if your company has achieved the seven elements of governance listed at the opening of this chapter and to affirm that the risk of financial misstatements has been substantially reduced.

Getting to good governance is both a value and state of mind. The value proposition involves the improved transparency that good governance provides. The state of mind comes from knowing that, done properly, good governance improves the effectiveness and efficiency of the company.

Good governance takes a number of forms:

- Accounting for the business and the subsequent financial reporting of that accounting
- Information technology systems and processes
- Board operations and decision-making
- How the business describes itself to investors
- Timely disclosure of all of this information, in compliance with SEC and exchange rules

Let's discuss and determine how to achieve these forms of good governance.

BOARD GOVERNANCE

Selecting board members is critical. They need the right skills and background to add value to the company on an operating basis. But they also need the proper moral values to set the tone at the top of the company that, in turn, helps ensure proper governance throughout the company.

Thus, the very first board action should be to establish the moral and operating standards of the company, making sure they are shared both by board members and by the CEO. These standards should include more than just shared values; they should include a commitment by leadership to consistently abide by them. This agreement sets the tone at the top for behavior throughout the organization. It also establishes procedures for the implementation of corrective actions when things go astray.

Preparing some mission statement that is all too likely to be ignored is not enough. It must be backed up by real action—not just because it is the right thing to do, but because, particularly with a public company, there will be a number of third parties testing and searching for proof of action throughout the organization.

Moreover, for individual board members, these rules of behavior set a standard for being recruited to and remaining on the board and for being affiliated with the company. Among the attributes of proper board behavior should be independence (that is, precise rules on conflict of interest), good behavior both inside and outside the company, and requisite experience and skills.

The last will help the company determine both eligibility for the board and to which committee each new director should be assigned. The two most important board committees are audit and compensation. Not only must board members assigned to these committees have the requisite skill sets, but they also must be free of improper influence—not least because the major stock exchanges have specific requirements for the members and chairs of those committees.

Setting up a public company board should begin about two years before the proposed IPO date, starting with the two most important roles to be filled, that is, the chairs of the audit and compensation committees. There are a lot of procedures and processes for each committee to put in place, and it is easier if you have a bit of a runway to get these actions done.

The first step in establishing these two committees is to write their charters to set their duties and boundaries, and to begin holding regular meetings as soon as possible. These early meetings don't need specific agendas. Just meeting to discuss their progress with the governance game plan is important. Setting up documentation for executive compensation and describing such compensation is not a one-meeting adventure.

Also, it is important that outside, independent directors learn the business quickly so they can start adding value to the company. This is especially true for the committee chairs.

Further, it is important to get the meeting calendar set a year in advance, if not two years out. While members can attend remotely, it is best if the committee chairs and at least one committee member are at the company in person. Establishing this routine is important.

Once you start to form the board, look back inward to the business and its operations to start the process of proper operational governance.

ACCOUNTING AND FINANCIAL REPORTING

This work, to a large degree, is the basic blocking and tackling of good business practice. So it is amazing that, for some reason, this work is often not done during the start-up phase. That is a dangerously shortsighted approach; the longer you wait to set up these processes, the more you ultimately will spend on consultants and others to help you catch up for the time you've lost.

The process of implementing accounting and financial reporting starts with very basic questions:

- Are each of the accounts reconciled by an accountant?
- Is that reconciliation reviewed by another person?
- Did that person sign and date when they conducted the review and note any corrections that took place?
- Was an asset inventory done recently, and is there a proper record and listing of those assets?
- Does that inventory provide details such that a third party could find and identify a given asset?
- Are the assets listed being depreciated properly?
- Is the depreciation life set properly?

These questions may sound mundane, but it is amazing how few companies perform even these simple and basic steps.

Usually you'll find that the accounting department of a business with $40 to $50 million in revenue employs two to five professionals, all of them crushed by their workload. Needless to say, when you're so understaffed, details regularly fall through the cracks. Governance is an afterthought.

The first step, then, is to get the team staffed for success and put basic processes into place, all while tacking toward governance. That includes initiating the practice of peer review and the management review of account reconciliations. More often than not you will find an array of expenses sitting in unreconciled balance sheet accounts and unreconciled bank statements—that is, stuff you don't want your auditors to uncover as you prepare to go public.

This is one reason why, before we even start to think about going public, I change the year-end date and force an audit of all accounts. Simple concepts, such as month-end cutoffs, seem to always get lost in understaffed accounting and finance departments. In particular, a cutoff at month's end is both a major governance area and a critical matter of financial reporting.

At one company we found more than two thousand accounting adjustments and close to $3 million dollars in errors and cutoff issues. Our subsequent adjustments significantly lowered the growth trajectory for a few quarters—a painful reminder of why you want to do it right the first time, with good governance.

The governance aspect of accounting and finance should be apparent—it is about ensuring legal and proper adherence to accounting concepts and controls. It starts with documenting each process in accounting: how you pay bills, how you do payroll each month, how you receive payments from customers, how account reconciliations occur, who reviews them, and so forth. Are there documented indications that each of these reviews and controls is in place and being performed? Who conducted the review and when? What actions, if any, were taken with the results?

If these processes are not put in place early in a rapidly growing company, things can get messy pretty fast. To remedy this, I focus on three areas of accounting and finance:

- Expense reports
- Compliance reports
- Metrics

1. Expense Reports

You need to prevent employees just stopping by to drop off their expense reports accompanied by a stack of receipts (or worse, without them). There are two actions I start immediately because they involve the whole company and help set the tone for further changes down the road.

First, we announce we will only reimburse for expenses incurred in the past sixty days. For adhering to that policy, we send a note to employees thanking them for their contribution to the company and informing them that in the two years we have had the policy in place there have been only thirty violations of the sixty-day rule, and the company has collected or saved $10,000. People learn quickly and the word spreads. The early violators are generally the executive staff, as they may assume the policy does not apply to them. But the first time they don't get reimbursed, they understand. Also, we do not have company credit cards. While the company will pay for the annual fee on a card, the card remains in the employee's name, so they are on the hook for unpaid and past due amounts.

This sixty-day policy is important for a couple of reasons. Imagine an employee sits on expense receipts that add up to more than $75,000 for nine months. (This actually happened.) Needless to say, it puts a real burden on the accounting department, because of both the work required to validate those expenses, and the impact to the monthly reporting data.

Now, I have to say, like most people, I hate preparing expense reports. So once I have the process basics in place—sorting out the timing of submissions, remembering to get receipts, and recording the business purpose—the next step is automation. Make it easy to report expenses, and the expenses are more likely to get reported on time and accurately.

The good news is there are many inexpensive and effective T&E solutions available these days. I look for those solutions that allow the user to photograph the receipt on the spot, add details, and push a button to create or add to an expense report. Add this automation to a workflow path that facilitates the approval process on the other end, and I'm happy. So are my fellow employees, because with this, I can comfortably move the expense reimbursement process from sixty to thirty days.

This change usually incurs a certain amount of whining, but I've learned that if I hold firm, the company culture will change. Otherwise, as the company grows, unfiled and unpaid expenses quickly mount into the millions of dollars—significant enough to create misstated financials and other serious consequences.

Most companies fail to put in place proper review and controls for purchases. As a result, anyone with a credit card can buy anything and just present the bill to finance for reimbursement. But this isn't the buyer's money; it's the company's. So the buyer is in no hurry to take care of the paperwork involved. They've made the purchase, they have what they need, and reporting the process is a secondary distraction. The challenge then is to get all company employees to act as if it is their money.

To mitigate this, I have used solutions like Coupa, a procurement cloud product that introduces the concepts of purchase orders, management approval at all levels of the business, and spending approval authority. With this solution on board, while folks throughout the company can spend money, they cannot spend it in advance of management approval, which I limit to the most senior executives. This places accountability and responsibility upon the executives and helps everyone understand cash is precious, not to be spent on an impulse.

Further, these changes begin to educate the entire company about controls and governance. Two interesting features of a procurement and purchase order solution like Coupa are that it adds control workflow to your purchasing process, and it provides an online store, aggregating numerous items so that even a small business can get the best pricing on standard office products. This is one example of a cloud solution you should look for to enhance workflow controls and make SOX controls compliance easier.

Overall, the best approach to corporate governance is to set up processes as if your company is bigger than it is currently. That said, change management is always hard, but especially so if you are attempting behavioral change. The sooner you make certain fundamental changes—such as approvals and spending controls—the more effective they become and the easier it is to grow and add new employees.

The biggest obstacle to institutional change is the status quo, the "but this is how we have always done it" attitude. That's why the sooner you get these processes in place, the more time everyone has to adapt to the change.

One company I joined had no such controls. The controller was putting company charges on her credit card and making the payments herself. Management did not want to be bothered with the purchase details or with putting a control process in place. As a result, they were clueless about the company's true cash flow. This is pretty typical for start-ups. However, getting control over cash spending should be a top project from the start.

What employees see as merely a single Starbucks coffee each day, a CFO sees as the cumulative cost of hundreds of coffees every day, and none of that expense generating a penny of return to investors.

I did finally manage to implement a procurement system at that company, but the complaints from both rank-and-file and management were endless. I held my ground—after all, I had to be accountable to our investors for where our money went. In the end, that company had to go public simply because it was running out of cash.

Once again, documenting and putting into place accounting and reporting process controls is a first step to running a viable business, whether you are public or not.

2. Compliance Reports

The second attribute of governance is the timely and accurate disclosure and filing of company reports. This includes the creation of compliance reports, such as

- Tax returns
- Employee benefits
- Workers compensation benefits
- Other state and federal filings as required by law

Every company, private and public, must make these filings. However, for a public company, there are filings required on a quarterly and annual basis. They include:

- A registration statement (the S-1)
- Quarterly filings (10-Qs)
- Annual filing (the 10-K)

There are additional filings as well, such as 8Ks, which report important new information about the business. The reason for filing an 8K could be as simple as bringing on a board member or hiring an executive vice president of marketing or sales.

The biggest challenge in all of these filings is timing. There are prescribed deadlines set by the SEC that must be adhered to at the risk of a fine, or worse. Determining these deadlines is easy; meeting them is harder. That's where good governance applies. You will need people, processes, and review for sign-off to get the job done on time.

To accomplish this, you must hire the right people to get accurate numbers in a timely way—that is part of the accounting and legal process you must set up internally. Also, you must find outside legal and audit support to help with the details of the documents and to ensure proper review.

I typically will look to hire the best SEC accounting person I can find, along with a veteran in-house SEC legal counsel. They must be able to work as a team, and they must be excellent at staying current with new requirements. Finally, they must help the company gather the necessary details to report in a timely and accurate manner.

Fortunately, the SEC has developed an emerging growth company (EGC) classification to overcome what many had seen as overly burdensome regulations for IPOs and public companies. It reduced some of the reporting requirements and allowed later adoption of accounting rules for companies under specific size and valuation guidelines. This has been helpful for early stage companies going public to mitigate some of the reporting requirements.

Though EGCs can delay some requirements, such as adopting new accounting pronouncements or new SEC or exchange requirements, I urge you not to wait to comply. Here's why: I listed Yext under the EGC rules, but I still decided not to delay fulfilling all the other requirements while we waited for a ruling on our qualification as an EGC. I'm glad we did—as it turned out, had we waited, we would have been screwed.

The requirement for regular companies is that new accounting rules must be adopted within six months after becoming a mainstream "accelerated filer." An accelerated filer is a company of a certain market cap that now has additional compliance requirements for adoption of new accounting rules and a much tighter time frame to file SEC reports. We petitioned in a number of places for a more sensible transition from being an EGC to being an accelerated filer.

The answer we received: "Sorry, you need to comply within the current fiscal year." The sad fact was that none of these agencies had really thought through the nature of this transition period and the challenges faced by a company trying to get through it. As a result, we had to adopt a wholly new revenue accounting pronouncement and be SOX compliant (attested to by our auditors) within six months of becoming an accelerated filer. That was a mere eighteen months from our going public.

In the end, qualifying as an EGC would only have given us a false confidence. We never would have made the transition in time. Thankfully, we had started in advance of our IPO to install processes and act as if we already were an accelerated filer.

Looking back, between the accounting changes and the presentation on adoption required, I am pretty certain that the needs of the investor were only partially enhanced and in some cases actually reduced. Now, I am a very big fan of doing accounting that reflects the economics of the business and not the theory of accounting. Sadly, as you move from EGC to accelerated filer status, it is the theory that gets in the way of actual business transactions being accurately accounted.

Why am I telling you all this? To encourage you to set your disclosure and reporting on the path to accelerated filer status, even before you go public. It will help you avoid some of the chaos created by regulatory and accounting bodies that may be oblivious to real-world consequences.

3. Metrics

Remember, you hired people to perform certain tasks. If you made great hires, all the better, but if you are on a growth path and want to manage your business, not just run the business, you need to determine just how well those employees are doing. That requires metrics and reports to determine the fit between their performance and your goals.

These measurement forms include:

- Financial reports
- Cash flow reports
- Cash forecasting

You can get these reports by installing information systems and technology. We have discussed this approach elsewhere—here, we will discuss the challenges to the operation of these systems.

CHANGE CONTROL

Anticipating the future of a company is tough. The systems you have put in place and the cloud that supports these systems make the work easier, but not simpler.

For example, the software solutions you have developed are going to be subject to "change control," a broad term well known in the audit and legal industries, but not often appreciated by a business.

Change control is a rather simple concept in theory; but implementing and maintaining it are not. The idea is this: when you change any of your existing software you need to do a few things before putting it back into use, including the following:

- Conduct a quality check for coding errors or system bugs
- Run any changes in a "sandbox," a simulated working environment that replicates the impact the change will have on your existing products and processes
- Make sure the new change does not create any unanticipated downstream effects that produce new errors
- Undertake a code review by someone other than the person or team who wrote the new code to ensure the changes make sense
- Have the code review team sign off on their work after all the above has been completed

- Establish a process to implement the new code into the live systems and processes
- Have your quality assurance folks make sure the change actually works as intended in the real-life environment
- Maintain records of all of the above
- Describe the operation of the changed functionality of the system in a document for future operators
- Identify any behavioral changes that must occur among the operators of the modified system and incorporate into their management and performance measurement

Sounds straightforward, doesn't it? Yet every company I have ever worked at ends up making their process changes on the fly on live production lines or on live software code. Hey, I mean, who maintains a second code source for anything?

Of course that means bugs are discovered when things go awry, the whole company essentially shuts down, and code writers heroically scramble all night trying to fix the problem before customers discover the disaster the next morning. Worse, if they fail, the customer gets to discover that a change has crashed the whole system. Did I say "customer," singular? Imagine two to five hundred furious customers who will now never quite trust you and will question your competence ever after.

The point I'm trying to make here is this: while it seems easy to make this change, the unintended consequences can be horrendous, including lost data, lost time, lost money, lost reputation, and ultimately, lost business. You do not want to go down this path.

BUILD IN CONTROLS

There are two categories of controls with which you must deal. They can be leveraged, but they will cross most areas of your business: control testing and Sarbanes-Oxley controls.

1. Control Testing

The first, control testing, is what is referred to as SOC 2 controls. (In Europe they are called ISO controls.) These are audits and testing protocols that ensure your product team is following code release and quality testing. This is critical so that customers using the common protocols can rely on your testing and controls process. It also means that your company does not have to go back and test all the changes you've given those customers.

Regarding control testing, I want to share two notable experiences. In the first case, the original code for our company's ERP system had been running for about three years. At that time, a problem had emerged: the system's rounding assumptions increasingly were causing an overstatement of revenues. After a few sleepless nights, we found the issue and made an adjustment to our financials.

The second case: a global T&E reporting system provider was discovered to be getting faulty SOC 2 audit results. This forced every one of its customers into getting a public company audit to go back—at great time and expense—to retest every one of their transactions to verify that their internal system was working properly. As one of those companies, in addition to proving our system outcomes, we also had to rehire our external auditors to check those tests. This was not an insignificant expense—one we have yet to recover from that supplier.

The truth is that I have never seen a company *not* have an IT systems control weakness. That means if you don't think you have a problem, you are likely mistaken, and you should take the time to look again.

2. Sarbanes-Oxley

These controls and testing programs are designed to ensure that no one can change values in a financial system that will materially impact the reported results. Such value changes are usually made by system administrators, software developers, and sometimes even end users. The same procedures apply here as to product developers. A protocol must be put into place in which any designated employee who proposes a value change must determine a way to safely test the change, sign off on the test, implement the change, and ensure that proper outcomes are noted.

Some control processes prove more challenging than others. The control process that most often fails is that of managing access to systems by newly terminated employees. If access by a terminated employee is not shut off quickly and completely, you have a problem. Terminated employees, sometimes irrational and vindictive, can create considerable damage. The combination of single sign-on and timely notifications between HR and IT is usually where the control breaks down.

Another common control problem lies in the difference between financial auditors and SOC 2 auditors. Financial auditors are focused exclusively on the accuracy of your financial data. By comparison, SOC 2 auditors are looking for compliance with your stated processes and controls. Your financial auditors are also focused on the impact these process controls and procedures have on your financial results. If they find inadequate controls and too many exceptions to the process controls described, along with unacceptable access to the systems, they will throw the results of your financial audit in doubt, even if the numbers are, in fact, accurate. That audit won't be usable until the SOC 2 folks are satisfied. This will result in a judgment by the auditor that you have a material weakness in your systems controls. Even though the financial numbers are fine, it puts into question the controls and creates a risk of misstatement of the numbers going forward.

Unfortunately, this occurred at one company at which I was employed. We worked the accounting department hard to check every number—not just one, but two reviews, to ensure we produced accurate results. For the most part we had succeeded, to great fanfare, because we had started with no records, with no real accounting reports, and it took months to close the books. We were hugely proud of ourselves. Sadly, material weakness in our systems and access controls negated all of our hard work. More importantly, it significantly impacted the amount of work the external auditors had to do, raising our audit fees and then raising our legal fees.

The good news is this: today's cloud solutions offer great workflow to build and document controls. If you start early, you can put in place proper access controls and eventually you can realize reduced audit fees.

The other thing to watch for in this process is the doubling-up effect of SOC 2 (or ISO in Europe) and SOX. You can be SOC 2 compliant but not SOX compliant. If you are neither SOC 2 nor SOX compliant, then it seems all is lost. Because in today's world of mitigating legal exposure, a failure in SOC 2 and SOX can be construed to mean your legal and accounting team can't file your SEC documents in a timely way.

In the modern company, no matter how small or big, every employee counts, and every person should be accountable. Every employee has the power to create great change or great damage. That's why every employee should raise his or her hand when they see something wrong—whether it is about failures of controls or behaviors that negatively impact the company or the workplace. All too often it has been left to someone else to act. At the end of the day, it is the duty of the company to educate every one of its stakeholders that every day, every dollar, and every decision matters.

TRADEMARKS AND DOMAIN NAMES

While procuring and managing trademarks and domain names does not, strictly speaking, fall under governance, these processes are part of getting your legal house in order. From the day you start a company, you should trademark important phrases or images, not just in the U.S. but globally. Similarly, you should register your critical domain names in all countries in which you expect or hope to do business.

Some people make a lot of money off buying and reselling domain names. When they see a company succeeding in the US, they register that company's domain names and trademarks in countries outside of America. Then, when the company attempts to procure those trademarks and domain names, they find themselves in price negotiations for their own names in each new country. Fair warning: once you do procure your names and trademarks, keep them current. If your registration lapses, you can lose your name once again, costing as much as $250,000 per country to get it back.

CHAPTER 7

THE BANKERS

A key factor in going public, and then operating as a public corporation, is getting to know some very special financial institutions. These aren't your local bank or savings and loan, but the kinds of places most of us only read about. In going public, you become part of this new world.

Let's start with the basics: the various players you will interact with and how you will relate to each of them.

YOUR INVESTMENT BANKING TEAM

The first person you will meet will be a representative from your new investment banking team. This team is part of a larger group that packages and sells stock or deals to their customers, otherwise known as investors.

The investment banking team will help you negotiate the process of going public and help you sell your new stock offering to investors. Amusingly, they usually meet with you in packs. That pack includes the following:

- A number-one banker, or lead banker. This person is usually there only for show—and to serve as the last resort if you, as the client, have a problem.
- A number-two banker who will be your main contact. Get to know this banker—you will be working with this person a lot in the weeks ahead.
- A number-three banker, the equity capital markets (ECM) person. This person, you will be told, "knows the market"—how it is doing at any given moment and how to get you the best opening price.
- Sometimes this pack (and certainly the team) will feature a corporate debt person who will discuss with you alternative types of fundraising via debt, in order to give you "a complete picture" of your options.
- Inevitably, your team will also include a staff person—the person who works twenty-four seven, doing just about anything asked of them. This person aspires, if they survive, to be a number-two banker someday. Get to know this person because they will be on top of the latest developments in your case, though they will have no power to change anything.

The majority of the time you will work most closely with the number-two banker and the staff person. The lead banker will drop in and out as needed, typically providing advice or trying to change your mind about something to "improve the value" of your IPO.

Once you've completed the IPO, you will never see this team again, at least until the number-two banker and the ECM person reappear in a few years to pitch you on a follow-on offering or the issuance of convertible debt. When this occurs, they are no longer your business associates, but a sales team, selling to you and to investors. Treat them accordingly, always keeping in mind the quality of the work they did on the IPO.

YOUR RESEARCH TEAM

Your investment bank will organize a second group for you, your research team. This team has two sides. One is often referred to as the sell-side research. You will work with them up to the IPO and beyond. Every quarter they will contact you to ask questions in order to estimate your future value. To do this, they will use a wide array of models and methods and issue quarterly updates and recommendations to buy or sell your company stock. More on this relationship later.

Meanwhile, on the buy side—targeted at those who will buy your stock—typically you will have two folks: the buy-side research analyst and the portfolio manager (PM). There may, in fact, be a few different portfolio managers interested in your company shares, depending upon their fund's investment charter. It could be a growth fund, a tech fund, a long-only fund, a hedge fund, or any number of titles that indicate what they invest in and how long they invest. Again, more to come in the next chapter.

For now, let's talk about working with your bankers.

PREPARING TO WORK WITH BANKERS

Let's return now to the bankers and discuss what you need to consider before you agree to work with them.

First, you need to understand that bankers, of any size firm, provide pretty much the same services. Generally they cater to most of the same buy-side institutions, and they're in the business of selling stock. They all have trading desks where, daily, they meet the needs of buy-side institutions.

When they come to meet with you, they will all provide a twenty- to thirty-page leave-behind document listing the resumes of the team, details of their most recent IPOs or funding activities, and historical data tweaked to show they are number one in their business (by some metric specifically chosen to their advantage). They also will arrive with a variety of techniques to "estimate the potential value" of your company—typically by comparing your company to businesses that may or may not relate to your own. The age-old cliché that you can prove anything with enough data points massaged the right way will be in full force. Proof by selective demonstration, it's sometimes called.

To mitigate this, you should start constructing your own list of public and non-public companies with which to compare yourself. This list should be based upon a shared business model or a common industry in which you compete. These are the companies you should look at for comparable valuations as you develop your own analysis.

In determining valuation I make sure I work from a core group of three to five comparison companies. Of course, every business is unique, but it is also true that there are always direct competitors and near-direct competitors to look at and understand how they are valued.

At Salesforce, finding this core group was pretty easy: we were in the CRM business-to-business (B2B) space, so we could look at Oracle, Microsoft, SAP, and Siebel Systems. While they were much larger than Salesforce at that point, those companies gave me an idea of what we should look like from a financial model standpoint and to whom sell-side and buy-side research would compare us. These comparisons also showed where we would be different and provided insight into how a multi-tenant business model would look compared to existing software companies. (At the time, multi-tenant was the term used to describe SaaS and cloud computing subscription business models before these terms became popular.)

In the Salesforce case, not only was our multi-tenant model a new approach, but so was our overall business model, which used a subscription approach to software. Our potential revenues were more predictable than a one-time software sale, given this subscription offering. To raise the value of Salesforce stock, we understood that we would need to explain both the multi-tenant model and the subscription approach.

The lesson here is that it is important to identify your similarities and differences with your comparison companies, as this will be a key point of discussion with all the constituencies involved as you go through and beyond the IPO process.

We went through a number of draft descriptions of what Salesforce was, starting with "multi-tenant computing" then "utility computing" and finally, as the industry became established, "cloud computing." These draft descriptions were important for describing our competitive advantage. They were also helpful in distinguishing our business model through deferred revenue, sales productivity, and cash flow.

It is critical to do this homework before you get bankers or research involved. You must know yourself first before you try to get others to know you.

The other bit of work we did at Salesforce—and I still do this with Yext and the benchmark companies we follow—is to go back and do comparables between your company and the benchmark companies you are following by looking at their S-1, or registration filing. Every business evolves over time, in scale and geographic footprint. So with those companies, go back to when they were the same relative size and scale as your company is now. Now, compare yourself and your business model to those benchmark companies.

It always is amazing to me that the research folks don't do this simple benchmark themselves, since they have all of the historical data at their fingertips.

What we found in doing this research with Salesforce—that is, comparing our business results to Oracle, SAP, and Microsoft for the same first five years of their start-up and IPO—was that we actually were growing faster and getting profitable quicker than those companies during the same period of their life cycles.

Meanwhile, the sell side insisted on comparing Salesforce to the current incarnation of these multi-billion-dollar, twenty-year-old companies with no growth and in a period of the life cycle where they were maximizing profits. For example, at this point Oracle was putting up nearly 40 percent operating margins while growing less than 5 percent. With those numbers they should have been emphasizing operating margins. By comparison, at three-year-old Salesforce, growing at 60 percent annually, such a comparable made no sense.

This experience points to one other piece of advice: know your sell-side research. What I had finally realized was that the research folks I was dealing with had not been around when Oracle, Microsoft, and SAP had gone public. They had no frame of reference. Luckily, there were a few people on the sell side who did understand the problem, and we were able to convince the others to take a second look.

At Yext, since we were creating a brand-new category, finding an accurate comparison was a bit harder. Since a direct comparison was not available, we compared aspects of other businesses instead. We looked for businesses with similar business models and similar-style selling approaches. Given our subscription business model and direct sales approach, we selected a group of companies (including Salesforce) when they were at our current size and scale. Making sure you compare each company at the same approximate revenue scale allows you to benchmark business models on a comparative basis.

To do this, you can compare relatively simple metrics such as:

- Revenue
- Revenue growth rates
- Sales and marketing as a percentage of revenue
- Product development as a percentage of revenue
- General and administrative (G&A) as a percent of revenue
- Gross margins
- Revenue per head
- Operating margins
- Cash flow per share

All of these can give you a good look at how your business is the same as—and, just as important, how it is different from—your peer group. They also help you better understand areas for improvement in your business.

Once again, these comparisons are all time-phased for revenue size and time-to and time-from IPO. I use these comparables all the time to help center our current annual performance and also with senior management to help in the business management and investment discussions when we are preparing budgets.

There most certainly needs to be an improvement in financial metrics for these comparable businesses every year. It is critical to long-term success. It also helps model where you need to be as your growth slows.

Where Oracle may have raised operating margins to 40 percent when it had no growth, I think 25 percent is about right for a software company experiencing slowing growth. Flow any additional margins back into the business to keep the business growing in the 5 percent range.

Ideally, at this point you know your company better than you ever have. Now you are ready to talk to the people with money: bankers.

ENGAGING THE BANKERS

Once you have a thorough understanding of your business and business model, it is time to start to engage the bankers.

I suggest you get to know the sell-side research folks first. You can expect to have a long relationship with them, while the bankers will leave after the IPO.

Here are some characteristics of excellent sell-side research people:

- They get your story. They understand your approach to what you are doing and the value-add or game-changing product or solution you bring to the table.
- They ask good questions. Even more, they learn the right answers. They'll need that when they explain your story to customers.
- They can adapt. When things go off the rails a bit—or a lot— they will be able to provide an informed analysis to their institutional investors.
- They can communicate. They can go on CNBC or Fox Business and cogently explain in business terms what your company is doing.
- They can evaluate. Great research people have a gift for combining both the empirical and the subjective to determine accurately the underlying valuation.

I have known some great sell-side analysts. These folks did their research. They called customers or prospects (even those who did not renew their subscriptions). They attended company conferences not just to meet management, but to meet customers and understand what issues they might be having with the company's execution or solution. And they were superb storytellers. These are the sell-side research analysts you want to find.

The alternative is what I call the spreadsheet jockey. This type simply looks at the math and often misses emerging trends. As such, they are almost always accurate, but not always right. Steer clear of these folks.

Early in my career, one of my managers made this lasting comment: "Finance is never about the numbers; it is about what is on the production line that reflects in the numbers." At the time I was doing inventory accounting at Hewlett-Packard, my first job out of graduate school. My job was to ensure proper inventory amounts at the end of each month and then to run the semiannual physical inventories to ensure we had less than 1 percent delta, plus or minus, to what was reflected in the financials.

That manager would walk me around the production floor and show me where the excess inventory or bad parts might be found. We walked through the inventory cages to check on the parts bins and see which were full or overflowing with parts and which were empty. The whole point was to perform a reality check, to learn from what I saw on the line—the quantities of spares or bad parts and the stock levels in the stock rooms. We could then translate that information into understanding if the inventory was going up or down and the estimated changes I expected to see in the financial statements.

This is important in any financial role: it is not about the numbers on the paper; it is about what you see in the business that is reflected in those numbers. If you don't know the story, you can't tell if the spreadsheet is near reality or not.

Most often the spreadsheet is far from reality. If you apply that less than 1 percent error deviation, it's obvious that you simply have to become more observant, more understanding of the real drivers of the business, and more tuned in to surrounding factors that won't be reflected in the spreadsheet.

In short, there is the science of numbers, but what really counts is the art of those numbers. That art is the key to a successful business.

Think of it this way: HP invented and improved upon early chemical analysis machines. Its new models could tell all the chemical components in a liquid. That's the science of it.

Well, wine is a liquid. So if you knew all the chemical elements of a great wine, you could simply combine the ingredients and make a great wine, right? If this were the case, my winemaking family could stop growing grapes and switch to chemistry to make its products.

Of course, that doesn't work. Empirically, a purely chemical process sounds good, except that, in real life, chemical analysis always shows the presence of "trace elements." Those trace elements make up the art of wine. Without them you simply get fancy grape juice.

Sadly, the spreadsheet jockeys miss the art of a business—which is what any great enterprise is really all about.

What happens when the science of numbers outpaces the art in business? In the late '70s and '80s, General Motors was known as a great car company. The company also had a fantastic financial analytics function. In fact, it was so good that over time that function assumed an ever-greater decision-making role in the company. In its new role, it began to impose more and more metrics and key performance indicators (KPIs) on the business.

Needless to say, in the process GM lost the art of making interesting new cars and features. It became known as a company run by bean counters who put profits over customer desire, and who were running the business into the ground. It took twenty years for GM to recover.

In a business, start-up or otherwise, you need to be careful with analytics. You can measure the business, sure, but I caution you against allowing those numbers to confirm your biases, or to stop you from listening to your customers.

If you find yourself working with a sell-side research person who only asks about the numbers, and then more numbers, and the details of all of those numbers, move on. You don't always get to pick who covers the company after IPO, but you sure can choose those people at IPO. So choose those professionals who understand and can repeat your story, and who can look through different lenses to value your company.

When you find that kind of person, help them up the learning curve. Make sure they get to meet the senior leadership team—the founder, CEO, marketing leadership, sales leadership, and financial leadership. Don't just make those introductions at a formal IPO organization meeting, but rather one-on-one, and in different venues.

The goal is to ensure that the sell-side person truly understands your story, where the business is headed currently and in the future, and its personality and culture. The last can only be conveyed in informal settings and through personal contact.

Begin this acclimation process early. At Salesforce we started about four years before the IPO. That may seem like a long lead time, but it was important for us to learn who truly understood what we were doing and who did not. Equally important, we regularly met with a core group of these folks once every four months so they could see how we were progressing, what issues we were struggling with, and how we as a management team resolved these issues.

I think this was one of the critical aspects of Salesforce's success: finding a number of really good sell-side research folks, most of whom ended up on the cover of our IPO prospectus as following us. They knew what we were capable of, even if we misstepped.

While it took many months to prepare for and conduct those meetings, it proved to be one of the most important aspects of getting our message out to our prospective and current investors.

Unfortunately, I haven't been as successful over the years with our lead banks. That's because the banking teams inevitably have more spreadsheet jockeys than storytellers. Thus, each time I have taken a company public, the lead bank sell side has placed a hold on the stock and at a lower stock price than the current market value. They seemed incapable of telling our story.

Having watched the banks screw this up to various degrees with all three companies, my only suggestion is that you pick your banks solely on your experience over time with the sell-side research person (not team) who will actually cover you. Even then, there is no guarantee of success. I have been baited-and-switched by the lead bank with a promise to have a certain person assigned to me, only to be shuffled off to someone else who didn't get the story.

Remember, the banking function is the same across all banks, but the sell side is not. Pick the best sell-side research folks you can and put them on your prospectus cover to take you public. One more caveat regarding sell-side research: researchers go to market, so make sure you understand the target investor of each of your sell-side people.

You will find that there are basically two types of investors: long investors and short-sellers, with many shades in between. See who your sell-side research person targets. I have known some really great sell-side research folks, but they mostly cater to short-sellers and hedge funds. So their commentary, even if done well, reflects a negative case for the company: why the competition will crush you, why a few customers have had a bad experience with you, why your business is declining, and so on. They cater to and create the "bear case" on your stock and as such can put your stock under heavy selling and price decline pressure. You don't want that kind of attention. So pick your sell-side researchers wisely.

HOW THE BANKERS REALLY HELP

As I explained, the bankers will meet with you in packs and provide leave-behind packages by the dozen so you can hand them out to the board and management.

Eventually they will meet with board members, management—and anyone up to six degrees of separation removed (sometimes more)—to help influence your decision to choose them not only to be part of your IPO but, more importantly, to hold the highest position they can to get on the cover page of your registration.

It's all interesting, but not very useful. You may learn the current state of the capital markets. But to be honest, no one really knows where the market is headed, other than directionally, most of the time, and you can get that information from cable news, without the dozens of leave-behind packets.

One way the bankers do contribute is to assist (not without considerable oversight on your part) with building the business section in the S-1, which in turn will somewhat inform the pitch deck for your road show.

I will say the best thing the SEC has done recently is allow for a "testing the waters," pre–road show. We had the opportunity to do this at Yext, and it helped significantly with regard to messaging and raising awareness within the investment community.

When it comes to selecting a lead bank—sometimes two co-lead banks—my general approach is to work with my company board of directors. They help get the banking team up to speed on the company story, so they can help write the business section. I tend to do this only after our in-house and outside legal teams have prepared most of the rest of the S-1 registration document. Of course, the underwriter's legal group can review the document—as can any other bank on the cover—but most law firms that have done an IPO have sufficient experience to get most of the registration done before you select your bankers.

We did not use this approach at Salesforce, and it took almost three months to complete the S-1. Imagine twenty or thirty people sitting in the same room, reading the same document, at the same time, and questioning if there should be a comma or a word changed or a hyphen added, and if we should leave this comment in or take this risk factor out because the world would have to come to an end before that scenario became a reality . . . and on and on. I wouldn't recommend it.

By comparison, at Pandora we had outside legal working with the company to prepare a draft of the S-1. We then used the lead bankers only to craft the story. With this approach, the S-1 was completed in thirteen days. At Yext we did it in about fifteen days. Thus, we saved significant time and spared ourselves a lot of frustrating, useless meetings. Lesson learned.

Do the S-1 draft work with outside counsel. Then let the banking team help craft the story of the business. The value-add the banking team brings is knowing their customers and knowing how those customers will respond to certain concepts, words, or turns of phrase.

The other component the banking team can help with is the road show pitch deck—the presentation you will give to potential major investors. Again, the team's value-add is its understanding of how their customer will react to certain language and visuals.

I also look to the bankers (or an outside investor relations consultant) to help train the management team on public speaking, responding to questions from a large group, and dealing with appearances on live TV. Most of my CEOs have already been very good at all of this, so the training was limited. Still, we both tuned up the message and really focused on Q&A.

Pandora was not so lucky. On IPO day we made a big mistake. We let the board of directors be on the floor of the exchange for the opening bell, and each one of them became new content for the on-air press team. Each was asked the same question, which at the time we really

weren't prepared to answer. We had nearly seventeen minutes of uninterrupted Q&A from on-air anchors about why we were still losing
money and when we would or how we could ever get to profitability.
Another pair of lessons: be totally prepared for questions, not just on
the road show but on IPO day, and limit, limit, limit the number of
people who speak on behalf of the company.

Today, not in my worst nightmare would I allow a director to speak
on behalf of the company, unless the CEO was arrested or dead and no
one else was available from management.

SELECTING A BANK

It used to be the case, and is still true today, that a company will invite
in a number of banks to a bake-off to have them compete to manage
that company's IPO.

There are good things to say about that strategy, not least that by
looking at the range of offerings the company can learn an awful lot.
But a bake-off can be distracting and time-consuming. Frankly, if you
have done your homework and you know who you want for your sell-
side research, there is no need for a bake-off. Rather, you can ask to
convene a board meeting, make your case for the bankers you want,
and hold a vote to select them.

This takes a major burden off the company and off the bankers
themselves, none of whom want to say, "No, we don't want to participate," none of whom want to be rejected in front of their competitors, and none of whom want to go through rigorous preparation for
nothing.

Some folks will host a bake-off not because they truly want to
see what the different banks have to offer, but because they want to
appease a one-degree-of-separation relationship. In other words, you
have a relationship with a bank on another matter, and they expect
they have the inside track, but you want to let them down easy.

Again, if you have done your homework and you know who you
want to work with on the sell side, even such a fragile diplomatic matter will not warrant a bake-off. Just make your decision, inform the
winners, and let the other bank know the specific reason it wasn't

chosen. Given the shortage of truly great storyteller sell-side research-ers, it's easy to explain your choice to the losing bank. Maybe they'll recruit the right sell-side researcher in the future.

We actually did run a grand bake-off at Salesforce to get going with a banker. Then, after a lag of three months while we wrote the S-1, a number of players in the potential lead banks had changed. So we held a mini bake-off among the finalists to determine who we should select as lead. They all made some errors this round, but one bank did something so goofy it lost the opportunity even to be part of the IPO. In fact, I didn't work with that bank for years after.

In truth, a bake-off only shows the bankers that what you really want is the right sell-side research people. By law, those people can't participate in the bake-off, as there is a legal firewall between banking and research. I'm not sure this is a good law, but it has been in place for nearly twenty years, and it is not going to change anytime soon.

Remember: in a few weeks, the banking team will move on to the next deal, but your sell-side person may be with you for years. While your bankers will only want to fill out their spreadsheets to fulfill the letter of the law, your sell-side person is, hopefully, already in your face asking about your story and preparing your message to potential investors. Ultimately, the goal should be to pick your banking team based on the sell-side research person and move on.

WHO COMES FIRST?

Placement on the prospectus cover—this is one hassle you can't escape. Needless to say, every bank will want top position. Trust me, you will learn quickly how petty this process can be. Your banks will fight over the value of appearing on the left or the right (and maybe in the center) of that page, while also above and definitely not below other banks of the same size. I've learned there are only two good remedies to all of this squabbling. First, tell them that if they don't like the arrangement they can always drop out of the deal. (That's not going to happen.) Second, and better yet, work with an investor relations (IR) consulting group that does this type of work all the time and has all the historical facts to call out the banks on their various claims.

For investor relations, I have always turned to a good and long-term friend, Tim Dolan of ICR, but there are a number of similar firms. Tim steps in to handle these negotiations using his considerable experience to make a compelling case for the proper order of recognition. Believe me, during the frantic ramp-up to an IPO you don't need this distraction—especially because, while it means everything to the bankers, it means nothing to you and the company.

Off-loading this argument to a professional will save you days and sometimes months of inane conversation. I've sent cases of wine to Tim because after some of the transactions we have done together, if he doesn't drink, he should.

ONE MORE THING

One final note on IPO and even post-IPO: there are a number of international exchanges to consider listing on, either with your IPO, or more likely long past IPO. These would be the Toronto Stock Exchange, the London Stock Exchange, the Tokyo Stock Exchange, and the Hong Kong Stock Exchange.

There are a few reasons to consider one or more of these additional exchanges. If you have a significant customer base in any of the countries, a listing raises awareness even after you have listed on, say, the NYSE. Also, it affords a more geographic approach to your investors.

It seems more and more of the type of investors looking for game-changing companies and long-term investment approaches come from Toronto, the UK, Switzerland, France, and Australia. Being listed on their exchanges and catering to these investors broadens investor reach and the ability to tell your company's story. Of course, this takes time and incurs additional costs, but wealth is being created in many parts of the world these days, and catering to your customer and investor bases in their home countries and on their terms means additional access for both your company and the local investors.

CHAPTER 8

THE INVESTORS

In the last chapter we discussed the value of bankers and the importance of getting to know them. In this chapter, we will make the same argument for investors—indeed, in the long run they are just as important.

Connecting directly with your investors, getting to know them, and educating them on your company story are often-overlooked parts of doing business. First, when current investors can tell your story to members of their network, you get access to potential future investors. Second, your current investors enjoy a wide range of skills and experiences, which may prove helpful as you pivot the company to address new markets, modify your go-to-market strategy, or pursue future acquisitions.

FIVE KINDS OF INVESTORS

Keep in mind all investors are not the same; there are, in fact, five main categories of investors. Successful, enduring companies eventually work with all of them.

1. The Growth Investor

This investor is looking to get out in front of the growth story, believing returns are best at this stage. Further, this investor is willing to look at a company that is not profitable and/or not cash-flow break-even when they go public, though you do need to demonstrate to this investor a large and expanding total addressable market (TAM), as well as a path to both positive cash flow and profits.

2. Growth at a Reasonable Price (GARP) Investors

These investors are not as aggressive as the growth investor in the early-stage growth phase or risk profile. Nevertheless, they are looking at companies that are fairly valued yet still have growth potential—and that are already demonstrating profitability and positive cash flow.

3. Value Investors

For these investors, long-term growth is less important. Their focus is on evidence of improving margins. They value growth in earnings per share (EPS), as opposed to growth on the top line.

4. Long-Term Investors

These folks, many of them utility companies or mature, stable firms, are looking to provide a return better or equal to bonds when you factor in earnings growth valuation and dividends. They are more focused on dividend returns than anything else.

5. Bear Case Short-Sellers

This group typically focuses on bad news. They thrive on worst-case scenarios, often arising from unsubstantiated rumors, innuendo, and misconceptions.

MANAGING PUBLIC ATTENTION

Remember: people make money in the stock market when the stock price goes up, when dividends are paid, or (if they are shorting the stock) when the price drops. The biggest challenge for a company trying continuously to grow its stock price is that it can show results only once per quarter. Meanwhile, a lot can happen in those three months— events, both good and bad, that can require press releases, media contacts, public announcements, and a whole array of tools to attempt to speak to the public. Even if nothing important is happening, you need those tools to keep attention on your company and demonstrate momentum, without setting a high expectation on Wall Street that you may fail to meet.

Maintaining this visibility becomes especially difficult during the SEC-required quiet period, which begins when you put your S-1 on file with the SEC. The regulation states that, during this period, you may not conduct undue promotion that may influence the opening price of your stock. But you may continue the level of promotion you operated at before. This argues that you should set that initial bar high: talking a lot to the media, and through them, to the public, beginning at least a year before your IPO. Most companies fail to do that, and thus when they need the public's attention, that option is closed to them.

Speaking of public attention, here short-sellers pose an obvious threat. Hedge funds and short-sellers often spread rumors. They might make the bear case over a drink after the market closes or make a subtle (or not so subtle) comment to fellow traders during the trading day. At their worst, they underwrite fake news and pay for biased or poorly researched news articles or blogs to proliferate destructive rumors. This is an especially pernicious problem: often the hardest part of being a public company is dealing with the ongoing naysayers creating short-sell opportunities for themselves with no basis in reality.

That said, there are a number of ways to work with investors even before you go public to properly educate them on your story and the plans you have for the future. Over time, you can invite them to cover your company as it grows and becomes successful. The best way to do this is to gain their trust by being open and honest with them, including about your mistakes. That can be difficult—nobody wants to see their failures in print. However, your candor will all but guarantee honest and insightful coverage for years to come.

Creating that kind of trust and goodwill is like money in the bank, insulating you from the predators. At both Salesforce and Yext, a single directional change and a misstep lingered for years at our investor meetings, kept alive by the short-sellers and rumormongers. Worse, even though everyone knew who was promulgating these rumors, they still became an ongoing concern for our long-term investors. Moving on wasn't easy.

But we got through it. At the end of the day, results count, so the only real solution is to keep your mind on the task at hand and keep the management team focused on honesty: doing what they say and saying what they do. The longer you use this approach, the more you validate the trust your growth investors put in you with their early investment in your story. Moreover, for your value and long-term investors, your honest approach will serve up continuous examples that refute the bear case.

ATTENDING CONFERENCES

In the early days of both Salesforce and Yext, we spent time getting to know potential investors through tech conferences (big and small) that offered private companies a chance both to make presentations on their businesses and to hold one-on-ones with potential investors.

This type of forum is a terrific opportunity to judge the reaction to your story and to train management in everything from large group public speaking to managing questions and even closing deals. Participating in forums like these also helps you begin positioning the company within investors' minds. In addition, these events give management early experience in the numerous personal meetings they will soon have with investors, some of whom they will first meet at these conferences. Relationships count, and the more often you can meet a prospective investor the better chance you have of landing him or her, and the more buzz you will generate within their networks.

Conferences and industry events are also a good place to test the waters on upcoming shifts in the company's strategy—such as

Salesforce's shift to cloud computing or Yext's decision to let companies be their own source of truth for web search results. With potential investors present, you can test reactions, uncover any concerns, and most of all, soften the upcoming shock. After all, it takes time for folks to grasp the need for change, to understand the type of change, and then to adjust to the magnitude of change. You can accelerate the acceptance of that change by using these settings for a careful rollout. Often customers can't see the future of technology, but they sure know what they need in the present moment when they see it. It is critical for a company to learn what a customer needs. Yext is great at modifying its solution to meet the customers' needs today while laying the foundation for the future.

Attending these private and public tech conferences throughout the year also enables interested parties to follow your company's evolution.

One thing to note: do not wait for invites to these conferences. At Salesforce we started going even before I joined the company, and that gave us four years of attendance at these conferences and speaking engagements both to hone our message and to raise visibility of the company.

At Yext, we had almost a two-year head start. Unfortunately, we did not pursue the program consistently, as we were migrating our product and business model in a number of ways. That took a lot of effort and reduced our time for these events. That said, we did start to compile a list of investors we wanted to meet and build relationships with, and we assiduously worked that list, at conferences and any other occasions we could create.

UNDERSTANDING YOUR INVESTORS

While your bankers will drive a lot of the share allocations, you will have some influence on who gets your shares. Your goal is to understand who you want and don't want to sell your shares to. Your target for obtaining that knowledge should be the official pricing day of your IPO, which will occur a few days before actually going public.

Ultimately, knowing your investors is just as important as knowing your customers.

What kinds of investors do you want to avoid? Certain investors will not comprehend your solution. In this case, it may be too early for these folks to be investors. I have been frustrated at both Salesforce and Yext when we meet investors who don't understand our solutions and either don't invest when they should or invest and then agitate about the investments we make to grow the company.

I have had a few experiences where some investors did not invest in Salesforce because their spreadsheets told them we were overvalued at $1 billion and $10 billion. At $50 billion they finally invested because the business was undeniable. These same investors later admitted they missed the early investment opportunity in Salesforce, but they were not going to make the same mistake with Yext. Sure enough, they invested in Yext based on the company's story. All good, but as we made certain investment moves that did not fit in their spreadsheet, the discussions began. The point is this: know who your investors are, and know what they are looking forward to in terms of determining valuation. In some cases, you may suggest to a potential investor they should not be invested yet in the company.

I've also worked with truly wonderful investors who understand the business, trust the moves we make, and stay with us for a long time. These folks are really fun to work with.

The investors you want to obtain your stock, of course, should have a long-term view of your story, and that story should manifest itself over the investment timelines of those investors. How do you know who they are? To get this type of information, you can subscribe to a number of services, such as Bloomberg. About eighteen months out, start getting familiar with these services and the information they contain.

I always keep a list of top shareholders in my benchmark companies. This helps me better understand who helps to support and drive the value of the shares, the size of their holdings, and, most importantly, how quickly particular investors churn their portfolios.

This churn rate gives you some idea about how long they may hold your shares. You can map that information to the time frame you have to achieving major company milestones. Few, if any, investors hold forever, but if you can find institutional investors that have low churn rates and tend to hold stock for three to seven years (if not longer), you want to devote more time to them to discuss your company story and your vision for creating value over the long term.

At Yext, we had a number of investors that, given their investment strategy and goals, had told us that they were committed to long-term holding periods. They also were very aboveboard with us that, from time to time, they might take some profits by selling a modest number of shares. We respected that honesty, which underscored that they were just the kind of people we wanted as investors.

An interesting side effect of having such honorable and loyal investors is that it makes your management team even more committed to the success of their own company. This happens not only because you know you will need to answer to these investors (as opposed to short-sellers), but because they trust you not to let them down.

By the way, as you conduct these searches for high-quality investors, look not only in the US, but also Canada, Australia, and the UK. In those countries, don't let an American name—for example, Goldman Sachs Wealth Management—cause you to prejudge their behavior. In fact, such a firm in the UK or Canada may have a completely different approach to investment. I have had great success with these investors, as many tend to look at long-term trends and invest in these trends. Moreover, along with investing in management rather than just the spreadsheet, these investors typically invest in your company's story and the growth prospects.

In other words, they are just the type of investors you are looking for.

The flip side of this initiative is identifying which investors have high churn and play the short side of the market more often than the long side.

We had one fund manager who got to know us. He tried to school us on how our business model should be changed and what metrics to use. Needless to say, months later we discovered that he was catering to the bear case and was shorting and lending shares to other short-sellers. Thankfully, he soon got out of our stock.

Looking back, I still puzzle over his motivation. He likely would have made much more money had he bet on our success, rather than trying to sabotage us. Maybe he really did not like our story. Maybe he was playing us. He represented himself as working for a long-only fund, which was where he held our stock. But if we had looked more closely, we would have noticed that the fund also had a hedge fund operation. Not to mention that he had a personal history of comparatively short average holding periods. This is a common trick: the larger institution buys on dips and obtains a significant amount of the public float, then they loan the stock for short trades.

The lesson? There are wolves out there, and they are sometimes disguised not as dumb sheep, but as trustworthy and reliable sheepdogs. So look closely at the investors you let in. This has been the case at all the companies I have taken public, so I've come to accept that this is part of the dynamic of stock market trading.

That said, the truly bizarre thing about the investor I mentioned was that, even as he was betting on us to fail, he would call and rail at me about the volatility of our stock and its poor performance. Of course, his firm's investment approach—along with a few of the very large institutions that were doing the same thing—was the underlying cause of our stock surges and retreats. It was surreal. We were not in the market with enough good news to have a countervailing impact on the trading value of our stock. Until we could answer effectively, we were largely at the mercy of those folks who wished the worst for us.

This type of trading behavior most often happens after your IPO and before your news blackout or lockup comes off—meaning your potential response is constricted. As a company you simply do not have enough shares in the market to dampen this type of trading manipulation.

Every person in these institutions denies this sort of thing goes on, but if you look at their trading churn over time and at their short-term interest of your stock, and you see that a few institutions hold big positions in your public float, it may be that the portfolio manager on the fifteenth floor doesn't know that the hedge fund on the seventeenth floor is shorting your stock . . . but someone in that firm knows, and none of this happens by accident.

Through these periods it is important to continue working hard with your good investors to make sure they get the company's real story and understand what you're doing and why you are doing it.

Ironically, one of the rewards for their loyalty is that they can buy even more of your stock during these short-seller–induced dips and show even greater returns.

At Salesforce we went public at $12 per share. After our IPO we conducted quarterly road shows to continue to educate the market about what cloud computing was and where we were taking the business. The stock was $12, then $15, then $25, then $50 . . . and on and on. We were always overvalued. Today, at more than $600 per share after twenty years of trading, it can truly be said that both the short-sellers and the ever-careful spreadsheet investors missed some great returns. Even today, I still believe Salesforce offers more upside to investors. (Note: that is not investment advice. You should always check with your wealth advisor.)

The same has been the case for Yext. We are still in the wonder years of the Yext story. People trying to work spreadsheets, bereft of the art of a business, may not get it. But in the real world, the business keeps growing, and Yext's customer base keeps responding positively to the growing arsenal of solutions.

A word about international investors, the folks willing to travel halfway around the world to meet you in New York and spend time hearing your story, meeting your management team, and learning about your company values, how you assess employees, and when and how you make decisions: put simply, I have the highest respect for them. At the end of one of those meetings you realize you have dealt with some very thoughtful individuals. They look for long-term investments and get to know management; they ask thoughtful questions about management style and culture, and how one plans to grow the workforce while keeping important aspects of culture and communication.

Further, these individuals and firms provide thoughtful commentary about what they have seen in other circumstances, trying to help all of you win, not just them. Working with win-win thinking people is such a joy. Sure, if they do invest, at some time they may, for various reasons, choose to move out of your stock. But, if you have done your job, they will have reaped great rewards, you will have had some great investors, and both of you can move on as winners.

GETTING MORE SHARES IN THE MARKET

It may seem premature at this point, before the IPO. Nevertheless, you should be thinking about your post-IPO future. In particular, as you engage investors, how will you get more shares in the market?

The process of offering additional stock is not strictly part of the IPO process, as it comes after going public day. But it is a direct result of that IPO, because now that you are a public company it becomes, for the first time, a valuable and legal way to raise capital.

For that reason, I am devoting the rest of this chapter to this process in its many forms, offering a step-by-step explanation of how to conduct it effectively. Along the way, I'll give you examples, good and bad, from my own career.

So why do you want to get more shares in the market?

First of all, the higher your trading volume, the less likely short-sellers can control your stock. Keep in mind that, at any given moment, you will inevitably have 3 to 7 percent of your stock in short positions. You can live with that; after all, everyone has to play their bet on the company.

But a higher ratio of shorts will leave you with little control over your stock, regardless of your performance, with one exception: that you beat and raise your numbers every quarter. One of the best ways to get your stock price to pop after quarter end is to blow out actuals and raise the bar. That's hard to do every quarter, but every time you can beat the bear case, you will get a stock jump.

It is crucial that you keep your ear to the ground for both the evolving bear and bull cases. These narratives determine the questions you need to address to debunk the bear case and to reinforce the bull case.

Even more, knowing the bear and bull case for your stock price, and formulating your argument against the bear case, will enable you to prepare to offer more shares to the market. Here's a look at the different forms of secondary offerings and their strengths and weaknesses.

1. Follow-On Offering

This is also called a secondary follow-on. It takes place when your company is not selling any, or is selling few, primary shares to allow the company to absorb any offering costs, thus sparing the secondary shareholders from paying a transaction fee when they're selling.

The secondary shares usually belong to the venture funds that helped get you to this point. They now want, or need, to liquidate and cash out.

The alternative is for the company to simply sell, in a follow-on, primary shares to raise more capital. Each method has been done successfully, and the decision about which to use typically depends on the VC investors and their approach to stock ownership. In all three cases in my experience, the VCs chose to hold the stock rather than participate in a follow-on offering.

Either option should move your public float to at least 15 percent—or better still 20 percent—of shares outstanding.

In the case of Salesforce, we actually wanted to do a secondary offering to allow some of our early employees and investors to enjoy some liquidity and to obtain a much-needed increase in public float. But our lead banker refused to do such an offering. They had so little faith in the company and its prospects that they believed that the share price—then trading in the high teens to low twenties—would sink below the initial offering price and ignite a ton of shareholder lawsuits.

Because of that institutional resistance, we chose not to do an offering of anything, primary or secondary. We could do that because the company remained cash flow positive, so we did not need operating funds. Our big investors simply put in place stock trading plans (known as 10b5-1 plans) to get liquidity. A 10b5-1 plan is a trading plan that happens on a routine basis without influence from the investor, thus allowing them to sell stock during periods that might normally be blacked out due to inside information. Since the plan is based on a set of parameters and executed by a third-party broker independent of the investor and company, these trades can happen at any time, regardless of company performance and activity, thus allowing for a rational selling plan and not negatively impacting the stock price.

Salesforce stock was trading in the forties when the bank finally suggested we do an offering. Our answer? No way. No, because we no longer needed the cash, and no way because it was clear they did not really believe the story or the company.

2. Convertible Offering of Low-Cost Debt

At Yext, by comparison, we were clearly burning cash. But every year—as we said we would—we reduced our cash burn. We eventually went from burning roughly $2 million a month down to cash flow positive for the full year. That said, we still wanted to raise cash, as we had a huge potential in front of us, and we wanted more public float. However, to our VCs' credit, no one wanted to sell their shares in the public market, mostly because they believed that the market had not yet fully valued our story. Unlike Salesforce's bank, our VCs did understand our long-term value, and they still do to this day.

The VCs eventually distributed their shares to their limited partners for a variety of reasons, from tax planning to fund requirements to simply taking some of their profits off the table.

Eventually at Yext we attempted a convertible offering of debt. The reason? We were sensing that interest rates were going to rise, and the era of really cheap capital was coming to an end.

We learned a lot—not all of it good—making our way through the complexities of this type of offering. For example, it quickly became really clear that the biggest beneficiary in this process is your favorite investment banker. I remember when, while I was at Salesforce, the pace of company IPOs was slowing. In response, even with interest rates at 5 to 7 percent, banks were promoting convertible offerings as the best fundraising option.

We passed on the opportunity. I didn't do it then, and I probably wouldn't do it now, unless a large potential acquisition was going to require excess cash. Even then, why would the company you are buying not take stock if they are as committed as you are to the success of the combined company? I get the need to pay some taxes, but even that expense should be no more than 20 to 25 percent of the transaction.

In the end, Yext passed on the convertible offering deal for three reasons:

- Paying the bankers to do this work when the size of the debt seemed too high was difficult to accept

- The accounting requirements and the hoops we would have had to put our accounting team through not just once, but every month
- The SEC reporting and disclosures requirements

All combined to make it difficult to see any sense in this strategy. In addition, when preparing for the offering, we set target prices, did a lot of work, and then when we thought it was time to get bankers involved, we made a call to let them know we wanted to meet them about a secondary offering. But before we even met, our stock already dropped well below our minimum target price.

When making these decisions, use your game theory and play out what happens when the five-year offering (or if you get lucky, a seven-year offering) comes due. Yes, with a good stock you can issue shares and perhaps they will provide less dilution in shares. But the incremental cost to administrate and deal with the ups and downs of your company and market will cost them both an economic and emotional toll.

That is why it is not clear what makes a convertible debt offering a brilliant solution for anyone but the bank. By the way, "Don't worry; you most likely can roll the debt over" sounds simple at the beginning. But this type of rollover can be tricky at best, depending on the state of the stock market, the state of the company, and the state of interest rates. For me, it's just not worth the risk and the banker fees unless you have very immediate use of the cash and the high potential for return on that cash is greater than your convert cost.

By the way, keep in mind that you will take a hit on your stock price when you issue more shares—maybe 2 to 5 percent, solely from dilution. Worse, just from the noise in the market about additional shares—likely from the hedge funds and short-sellers—your stock temporarily may tumble close to an additional 10 percent.

A lesson from all this: when you have to make a move on a share offering, keep the number of bankers tight and hold them accountable for the target price. If the market itself decides to drop 5 to 10 percent, make sure your bankers already know your walk-away terms. If you do walk, remember that the bankers don't get paid either. Invite them to participate in a successful offering when the market gets more stable.

3. Bought Offering

Finally, another approach to offering primary shares is a bought (or block) offering. In this type of offering underwriters are presented with a proposal from the company to sell in one tranche X number of shares. They are invited to participate, and the broker is directly purchasing the shares from the company at a price the broker proposes (their purchase price bid). You typically engage two to three brokers, and at the end of the day each broker submits a bid to purchase the shares. At the company you either select the appropriate bid or you decline the bids. Each broker knows there are other bidders, thus keeping the price close to current market prices. The brokers themselves are then seeing what uplifted price they can resell the shares at and build a book. Should they win the bid and purchase the shares, they have a place to resell the shares overnight.

I like this technique, in part because it often costs less than a traditional follow-on offering. Bankers and some investors will tell you this is a dangerous approach, which probably means they don't think they will make as much money. It also means that this is a good model to consider. It certainly was for Yext.

So how does it work?

- *Start with the amount you want to raise.* Thus, the shares you are going to sell. It will probably be the same-sized offering you would do in a traditional follow-on or secondary.
- *Get your SEC paperwork in line.* It helps if you have crossed the time frame for being public, allowing you to file for an offering quickly, without a registration statement.
- *Select no more than three banks with which to work.* Make sure they each separately have the trading volume to process your trade. You can typically look at the exchange services and Bloomberg to see who is handling the largest trading volume.

Note: the downside of this bank selection process is you are not buying new research coverage, but that is illegal anyway. So technically, you can't buy your way to more research. It used to be that research coverage was an integrated part of working with an investment bank on an IPO. In today's world the research people and the investment bankers have to operate without speaking with each other or sharing information. I have been in meetings where we meet the investment bankers in one room and then go to another room on a different floor of the building to have the same meeting with the research folks. This change came about in the early days of the Internet, where the sell-side research people in conjunction with the investment bankers might overly enhance a company's opportunity. The bankers selling the stock and a research person promoting the stock at the same time with the same agenda to raise the value of the company seemed to be too much of a conflict. Thus, new laws established that research had to be done independently of investment bankers taking a company public.

Of course, you don't market your company or see any new investors. But after eighteen months of tech conferences, your IPO road show, and quarterly non-deal road shows, it is unlikely you will find any real new investors at this point anyway. Most secondary offerings are now marketed in one day and mostly via video. I question the value of these video calls from the company to investors. They're intended to promote the stock and sell the offering, but to my mind they only allow the banks to rationalize their 4 percent of the deal fee. Here is an alternative approach:

- *Put together an offering package* that explains the usage of the proceeds of the offering, the number of shares you are selling, and the eventual dilution after the transaction. Further, create a short bid letter to accompany this information, informing the bidders of the basic terms and time frame of the offering.
- *Note that your three chosen bankers are bidding*, and ideally they do not know who the other bidders might be.

These are the basics, but you will need to get your outside legal service to walk through this process with you. You'll also need to hire an underwriter legal resource, typically the week before you start this process. It's best if you use the same counsel for the underwriter that you used for your IPO, so they are familiar with the company. The underwriter counsel will do due diligence and prepare questions and answers for the bidders. There will also be a bidder call, in which each

bidder calls in, not knowing the identity of the other bidders. Let's talk
about that next.

SELECTION DAY

The big day gets started with a phone call to your selected small group
of bidders from either your CFO or one of the great investor relations
services that has done this type of offering before. That is the start sig-
nal. The day rolls out as follows:

- 9:00 a.m.: Board pricing committee call regarding go/no-go
  based upon the previous day's closing price and the indicated
  morning opening of the exchanges.
- 9:00 a.m. to 10:00 a.m.: Finalize bid packets and get ready to
  PDF them to bank contact.
- 10:00 a.m. to 11:00 a.m.: Reach out to your best contact at each
  of the three selected banks. Inform them they have an opportunity to participate in this deal and they need to indicate
  interest by noon.
- 12:30 p.m. to 1:30 p.m.: Upon acceptance by banks, due diligence run by underwriter counsel.
- Following approval, the bank participants have until 4:05 p.m.,
  or right after close of market, to place a bid via e-mail.
- 4:05 p.m. to 4:30 p.m.: Clarifications, if needed, of bid details
  submitted.
- 4:30 p.m.: Board pricing committee has a conference call and
  selects the best bid or no bid at all.
- 4:45 p.m.: Winning bidder is notified. The faster you can get
  to this stage, the better, as the winning bank will be on the
  phone once notified, trying to sell the shares. Often the bank
  will provide a resell fixed price. For example, they will pay $10
  guaranteed to the company, adding that they intend to sell the
  shares to the market at a fixed price of $10.50. The bank's job is
  then to line up buyers and ensure the offering is subscribed or,
  better, oversubscribed.

(Needless to say, there are underwriter agreements that have been signed and passed between the bank and business in advance of this day, and all have been reviewed by the underwriter counsel.)

After all this, you may choose to put out a press release, as required, about the size and amount of the offering. Within twenty-four hours, the funds should be transferred to the company from the winning bank.

Over the next few days, you will be talking to your new investors—and others. They will be excited for the company and try to understand how you will use the funds. These investors are your newest storytellers.

The other investors you will hear from will be pissed because they did not get a chance to buy the additional shares or don't understand why you took this more cost-effective approach.

At the end of the day, the block or bought offering is an effective approach worth considering. It keeps you, as a company, in better control of your fundraising outcome, rather than placing all of your outcome in the hands of bankers who take their 4 percent fee and a discount of 3 to 5 percent on the shares they bought anyway.

A FINAL MESSAGE REGARDING INVESTOR RELATIONSHIPS

Investor relationships are as important as your customer relationships. To establish a strong foundation for your company, follow these steps:

1. Stay directly connected to your investors as much as you can.
2. Find and develop relationships with those investors who understand—and who want to understand—your story.
3. Know the bear and bull cases, then continuously address the bear issues upfront and reinforce the bull cases through your actions.
4. Remember, always do what you say and say what you do. That is the real foundation of trust.

CHAPTER 9

GETTING TO IPO DAY

You've come a long way. By two months out, you have in place a solid board of directors that meets your listing exchange criteria for independence. Your auditors are well on their way to completing audits of the company's prior years. Also, you have worked through any accounting issues and identified the required five significant accounting judgments you will be disclosing in your S-1 filing.

At this point, you can feel the momentum—IPO day is coming fast. What's next? Let me tell you.

REVIEW COMPARATIVE COMPANIES

As CFO, one of your responsibilities at this point is to review all relevant and comparative companies and make sure you're not missing anything or out of touch with what others are doing. Specifically, you want to make sure that what you are disclosing as significant accounting judgments matches their disclosures.

The same comparisons should be done for your risk factors. The legal folks will come up with a list of most of those factors to disclose, but it still is important that you know what others are disclosing in this regard. Indeed, even after your IPO, you should continue with semi-annual comparisons to keep you current with these companies.

I would also encourage you to look for any SEC reviews or comments regarding these companies. This will give you insight into what you might expect from your impending SEC review. These reviews are part of the filing process and a regular occurrence thereafter, so stay on top of the SEC reviews of those other firms and know how those companies replied.

As you can see, my approach is that I do not need to invent what has already been done elsewhere. Sure, I may need to tune those actions for my company, but if there is a huge body of work already available, all I need to do is adapt it to my circumstances.

SCHEDULE YOUR FILINGS

By now, your systems should be up and working and you should be using them to close your financials. While perhaps you are not capable of a seven-day close, you should still be well on your way to closing your financials and getting SEC reports ready to be filed on a quarterly and annual basis.

At this point it is also important to start establishing with the auditors your expectations for filing your required quarterly 10-Q or 10-K. You need to get them thinking about how long they will have to complete any quarterly reviews and how long you want them to take to complete the full-year audit.

Usually, I look to get the Qs filed with the SEC by the Friday of earnings-call week. This puts all relevant information in the public domain in time to allow you to have conversations with investors regarding the information you have disclosed. Usually the 10-K takes about a week longer, so I like to get it filed by the Friday after earnings-call week. This also eliminates issues around subsequent events should something come up after the earnings call but before filing the 10-Q or 10-K.

So push your auditors for a schedule that meets your needs and shortens the cycle from the end of the quarter to the earnings call to the filing of your SEC Q or K.

PREPARE FOR SOX

At this point you should also be closing in on completing the documentation of your processes and controls in anticipation of the start of Sarbanes-Oxley testing. That said, there is no need to complete SOX testing immediately, as that is only a requirement on your next 10-K, after going public. So why start now, when you have to attend to many other things? Because it takes a fair amount of time to get processes documented and controls understood by those responsible for them.

So the key is to be prepared well in advance. As I mentioned in chapter 3, I recommend beginning this process eighteen to twenty-four months out, because it usually takes that long to be audited for process and controls. That said, a number of companies put this off until they go public. Just know waiting can make it difficult to succeed in becoming SOX compliant, and one risks getting negative comments regarding proper internal controls.

The real benefit to becoming and staying SOX compliant—especially regarding information technology general controls (ITGC)—is the reduction in audit hours and therefore audit fees. Enabling the external auditors to rely on system control requires significantly less work on their part.

Moreover, once the data is in the systems, you can assume it to be correct—no more accidental insertion of errors while the data is being transformed from one medium to another. Your own team doesn't have to chase as much paper to demonstrate accurate data and neither do the auditors. This can result in huge savings in administrative costs, not to mention reduced wear and tear on the finance and IT teams.

SET YOUR BELL RING DATE

One thing I like to do at about two months out is to pick the IPO bell ringing date. That means, by definition, the night before is the pricing date. This puts a stake in the ground for all of the players in the process. It also kicks off discussions with a few constituencies yet to be involved, including bankers, the exchanges, and the board.

Generally, I like to price the stock on a Wednesday night, for a Thursday first day of trading. That way, you have two days of trading before the weekend to give the stock time to settle down.

The first day of trading is not especially meaningful for drawing long-term conclusions about the stock's strength. But day two, and immediately beyond, can indicate how the shares will trade over the coming weeks and months. We will talk later in this chapter about specifics regarding the art of pricing your shares.

Once you have selected your go-to date for IPO, the fun begins.

The first step is to contact your bankers and start the final process of selecting which you will use to take you out. Experience says that the best strategy is to have a good mix of both large and second-tier bankers. As discussed earlier, make sure you select your banks based upon your sell-side research and those firms with which you have built strong relationships. This is key, because you are with your sell-side research folks every quarter, but with your bankers only once, when they take you public.

Aside from the selection process, when it comes to banks, keep in mind the economics of the transaction. You will pay the banking consortium a fee of 7 percent of the value raised. (Note that this 7 percent is rarely if ever negotiated, and it remains the same for every banker you speak with, but somehow the SEC doesn't consider this price-fixing.)

From there you will spend your days investigating both who is listed on the cover and which banks will get what fraction of that 7 percent. This negotiation can get a little crazy, which is why it is best left to your investor relations team.

On one IPO we dealt with six banks. At one point, aside from the lead banker, we were simply going to list the banks in alphabetical order. Of course, one of the bank's names started with a *W*, so they could not abide alphabetization. Eventually, they realized that their portion of the IPO fee was not worth losing over this issue. But, before they did, I spent ten hours on this one silly point of contention.

After you finally get your consortium of underwriters sorted out, the newly designated leads inevitably will argue that they should get a bigger slice of the 7 percent. You don't need to listen to their arguments—if they don't like the current arrangement, just pick a different lead, or co-leads.

As for having more than one lead, there are arguments for both a single lead or a set of co-leads. I've done both. In my experience, it really makes no difference except on pricing day. Having more than one bank in the room to discuss pricing can be valuable, even worth the hassle of having squabbling co-leads.

In the end, the truly key folks in this pricing process are the equity capital markets people. They provide the read on the stock market in general as well as the word on the street surrounding the offering. While sometimes they can throw out strange statistics and one-off comments, taken as a whole they will help inform the price you set your shares to sell for the IPO.

THE S-1

The next step is putting together your schedule for completing your S-1, the U.S. Securities and Exchange Commission filing used by public companies to register their securities.

By now you should have very solid data for drafting your S-1. This includes risk factors, financial statements, footnotes, and exhibits, along with the basics of the management discussion and analysis (MD&A), compensation discussion and analysis (CD&A), the business section that describes your core business, and a timeline. The S-1 also needs to describe the roles of each of the underwriters.

I like to have the lead bank, accompanied by in-house legal and outside counsel, work on the first draft with the company. This cuts down the time and limits the otherwise endless debate over commas, colons, and words.

Once this first draft is complete, the co-lead then is brought in to look with fresh eyes, help tune up the copy, and offer a third-party take on what you have produced. Allow about a month for this process and no longer. If you can do it in less time, great. Keep in mind that this section will live on in subsequent filings of your Qs and Ks, so be careful about your claims. They should remain representative of your business and should last for a few years at a minimum.

UNDERWRITER DISCOVERY

As part of the pre-IPO process, and once the group of bankers is selected, there will follow a number of group meetings to educate the banking team about your company. The discovery comes over the course of several meetings of different types.

The first meeting introduces the bankers to company management and to the business. You will typically do these meetings for two separate groups. First, you meet with the underwriters (or bankers).

It is critical the banking teams are all present at this meeting, as it will be one of the few times they will meet all of the management and get to ask questions about the business. Just as important, all the key company executives need to be present on the other side of the table to describe their functional operations, show key metrics, and discuss factors (both good and bad) that contribute to the company's performance.

Second, you will replicate this session separately with the sell-side research of your underwriters. This meeting will be more focused on numbers, of course, but will present the same information. This meeting also must happen in person, with no dial-ins on either side. Should someone have a scheduling issue, start the meeting by having a conversation about the level of participation and suggest that if the underwriter can't attend this meeting, perhaps the underwriter's cut should be reduced. After all, you should ask, how can a research person not go to this session if the underwriter truly wants to provide meaningful and thoughtful research?

This session will most likely last all day, so make sure you get it on your own team's schedule. There is no missing this meeting and no video conferencing by your side either. It is that momentous. Millions, even billions of dollars and, just as important, the future of your company can hang in the balance.

The content of this meeting will include in-depth descriptions of the company's organization charts, the backgrounds of the leaders in each function, key measures of the functional operations, an overview of upcoming events, and, finally, key issues facing the function. Transparency is crucial, but at the same time, the company must resist giving away competitive information. Keep in mind that, while everyone is under nondisclosure agreement (NDA), this information inevitably will make it to the underwriter's next deal or into the public domain. So be careful.

One of the key discussions you should have at both meetings is your calculation of the total addressable market and your evaluation of the competition. These are critical for both the bankers and sell-side research.

The other crucial item is your five-year plan. This plan should be delivered with a fair amount of detail and should be your best estimate of where your business will be at the end of those five years. You should already have that data at hand. I usually get the finance team to conduct a rolling, by-month, five-year plan, as a normal course of running the business. It is fairly detailed around business model, headcount, margins, cash flow, and capital spending.

That said, at the two meetings I generally only share details out three years, leaving indicators of expectations beyond that. Why? Five years out is a long time. Additionally, effectively you are providing the sell side with your guidance by quarter for the next three years, and they too can use these numbers to anticipate future performance.

Keep in mind that this will enable the sell side to conduct a discounted cash flow (DCF) valuation analysis on your company. While it is desirable to be conservative, that information can negatively impact your valuations as well. In other words, there is a fine line, and it is worth management team and board discussion before these meetings to determine where that line is placed between a conservative and a higher valuation. If you set your three-to-five-year numbers too high, you will forever be chasing yourself; set it too low, and you won't get a good valuation on your IPO.

Personally, I like to haircut our bottoms-up five-year plan by about 10 percent, and even then, as I said, I provide only a three-year set of numbers. Frankly, who really knows what is going to happen five years from now? Still, you should have a good three-year set of goals and some line-of-sight of the numbers.

Details are important for this plan-building, so take the time and have models. At Yext, our rolling five-year plan was updated every six months, and it incorporated our current results with our go-forward model.

Needless to say, this work wasn't just for the IPO. For its own purposes, the company needed to get more detailed over time as we learned the business and were able to model it more effectively. Those details mean items such as estimating facilities growth, head count (not just in total, but by function and then by city, to do facility planning), and estimated wages in each location for each role.

This rolling, five-year plan should be an ongoing effort and should be resourced as you grow. At Yext we began with two and then three people, and we expanded from there. We found it particularly fruitful to hire former banking analysts for this work, people who were burned out with investment banking, but trained to be thoughtful about their models. They could take this skill and evolve our modeling. I recommend this as a good place to start.

At Salesforce, we also maintained a five-year plan, but only at the profit and loss (P&L) level, not for the balance sheet or cash flow. One reason was my ignorance and lack of experience. On the day of the sell-side research meeting, the other side asked for the company's five-year model, which of course I did not have. I hadn't even conceived of the need for one. Frankly, at that point, it took all of our efforts just to prepare our financials and prepare the current year's budget—all while the company was growing at 60 percent annually.

I remember that day vividly: I rushed into Marc Benioff's office—we had just thirty minutes—sat down, and said, "Here is our top line, and here is what we need for the number of subscribers." Then we guessed what we needed for resources three and five years out. The result was a back-of-the-envelope P&L. We finished with minutes to spare, and, incredibly, time proved our estimates were off only about 1 percent. The bankers were happy, and we proved once again the old saw that lucky and good are both necessary conditions for growing a successful business.

I learned my lesson. At Yext we created and maintained, as I said, a rolling, five-year plan, one that ultimately focused us on the day we would get to $1 billion in installed base. Thanks to a lot of detailed assumptions and a continual updating of the model, after two years we were tracking pretty closely. More importantly, the plan helped us better understand where we were executing well and where we needed to get better. It has proven to be a great road map to the future and a valuable method to help run the business.

As I write this, in our third year, we have not only grown but entered a number of new markets. That means we will, over the next year, do a pretty complete review of our model. We also have, on my suggestion, brought in analysts from Wall Street to help add to the model's details.

SELECTING AN EXCHANGE

At the time, choosing a stock exchange seemed vital for each of my IPOs, but looking back it was one of the least important acts of the IPO process.

Keep in mind you can list your company on any exchange in the world, but the two largest and most visible exchanges are the NYSE and NASDAQ. In the past, the best way to choose between the two was to determine how you wanted trades in your stock to be executed: via a floor trader / market maker (NYSE) or simple transaction matching (NASDAQ). Initially, the fees would be higher with the NYSE, but every year the fees get closer and the services offered by each exchange grow more similar.

For example, both exchanges offer daily stock surveillance. This searches for weird or anomalous trading activity, which may indicate insider information trading or leaked confidential information from the company.

That said, the exchange selection process can be fun—meeting the folks at each exchange, seeing how they work, learning of any services they offer for the fees you pay, and getting a tour of the operations.

While the exchanges have many similarities, some differences remain, specifically how they can help market your company and the stock.

NASDAQ, for example, is in the heart of Times Square. It is all video and electronic activity, complete with a big display on the street. If you visit, make sure you stop in and watch CNBC live, just to see where the on-air folks work. I'm not sure how, in that chaos, any of them can maintain focus.

As for me, I enjoy the NYSE. It is the home and physically the birthplace of stock trading in America. The rich history of the exchange, and the high-quality folks I've met there, make the NYSE a great outfit with which to work.

The Salesforce listing went wonderfully, and the opportunity to meet Dick Grasso, who at the time had been long-term CEO of the NYSE, was very exciting.

As an aside, that was not the first time a Cakebread had been at the New York Stock Exchange. My parents were well known for holding wine tastings on the exchange floor after hours. When I was there on the floor with Salesforce, numerous traders let me know they had met my parents, asked how they were, and inquired about the next wine tasting. The coolest part, however, was meeting the security team at the entrance. They also knew my parents, and we had great conversations as I came and went before the Salesforce IPO.

Whichever you choose, I recommend you select your exchange early, as it drives some of the content and requirements of your committee charters, as well as your filing requirements. It also defines the nuances of such items as the definition of independence for your directors.

As always, the people you meet and will be working with are the most important factor in determining your choice.

THE BOARD'S ROLE

It is critical you keep the board informed of and part of the company's mission decisions.

Selecting the bankers, selecting the exchange, and eventually recruiting a pricing committee to help determine the final share sale price should all have active participation by the board of directors. But the board should also recognize that it is there in an oversight and advisory role; it should not slow down the decision-making.

1. The Pricing Committee

Regarding the pricing committee, you should get this group named and in place early—two to three months before the IPO—because you will go through numerous discussions about pricing the shares and other key topics. The pricing committee is usually made up of two or three key directors and the founder or CEO. While you won't finalize any decisions until pricing day itself, it is really useful to get the pricing committee and the full board discussing this topic to get aligned as much as possible.

As I have told board committee members many times at these pricing meetings, the public market will set the proper valuation for the company, and that number most likely will not be the post-money valuation from fundraising. Don't focus on post-money valuations; focus on a conservative price that allows new investors to make money in the early days after IPO.

2. Pre-Public Market Valuation

Keep in mind that raising additional pre-IPO rounds of capital creates a tension between existing shareholders' dilution of interest in the company—which they don't want—and the providers of funds—who want to get the most interest in the company they can. At the end of the day the settlement will arise from the pre-money and post-money valuation, and while related to the performance of the company, it actually bears little or no relationship to public market valuation of the company.

It is very much worth getting your banks to do their models, but honestly, they are not giving you good data either, since their agenda is simply to convince you to do a public offering. I'm being harsh, because they have liability issues as well should folks be misled by them. But the simple truth is that the only real pre-public market valuation is the one that you do when comparing your measures with those of your peer group.

Remember, you should have started doing this comparison starting about two years ahead of your planned IPO to ensure you book the proper stock compensation expense and have properly valued the stock options you are granting.

It should be noted that the SEC will review both your external and internal valuations to determine if your stock option pricing is correct. The downside of this is the potential taxes on employees if their options are undervalued and understated.

With regard to the SEC review of stock compensation expense, rely on your outside advisors and get them involved early. You may have a third-party detailed valuation of the company performed every ninety days to set options prices, but that means little to the final decision for the sign-off of your registration statement, or S-1.

In my own experience, this detailed work paid off in two out of three cases. In the third, the SEC said we should just assume a straight line from two years out to IPO day. My advice is that you have a third party do a valuation, do your own market comparison, and then look at a straight line from three years out. Finally, make an informed call with outside advisors and the board to get their ratification. Otherwise you risk delaying your IPO while you debate with the SEC the proper stock option prices, a debate in which they will only tell you they disagree with you, but they cannot tell you the proper price. This added two months to the IPO process on this topic alone.

One advantage of having the board involved at this point is keeping it on track. Understanding and participating in board governance like pricing and other detail activities sets the board up for understanding the consequences of the decisions they are making.

I remember at Yext, when I joined the company, the board meetings were pretty good. We focused on financial results, execution, and strategy. However, the last year before the IPO, and especially the two board meetings before IPO day, were tortuous, mostly because of the necessary document read-through of all the corporate details.

By the second of these board meetings, everyone was complaining, and the meetings were turning into legal sessions. Thank goodness we went public, if only to get past this part of the process.

My suggestion? Put board members on notice that regular board meetings will be held and the usual schedule of financials, execution, and strategy will be maintained. Meanwhile, the documentation changes can be handled by the appropriate committee, with recommendations to the board, and with votes held when needed via phone call or attendance at the committee meeting.

One mistake most companies make is continuing to have the full board make a lot of decisions that can be done by the audit, comp, nomination, and governance committees. Those committees can then simply report major items to the board for confirmation.

Don't delay delegating decision authority to your committees. Simple matters, such as stock option grants, should be done by the comp committee, not the full board. That said, there remain certain items only the full board can approve. Address these matters at specially convened meetings, so they don't interfere with the board's regular business.

If you can get the documentation process completed and the pricing committee named a good month or two before the IPO, you will have done well in getting the board ready to become a public company.

COMMITTEE MEMBERSHIP AND TRAINING

Two more items remain.

The first is determining the membership of each committee. Qualification should be based upon the exchange on which you plan to be listed. It's going to take time to vet all of the candidates, so start early, really early, like two years in advance of the IPO, when possible. Obviously, you'll have to wait for some of these selections until you have chosen the exchange. It is important to find committee members who can add value to both the committee and the company, and who have a strong personality fit with other members of the board and management.

The second item is just as important (and even more tedious), because it can keep the company out of lawsuits: having outside legal take the full board and senior management team through the concepts and pitfalls of what is known as the SEC's regulation fair disclosure

(FD). These are the rules for when and what you can disclose to the public markets. These rules came about as many management companies were hosting private dinners or meetings with small groups of investors and providing additional information about the business but not making it publicly available to all investors. This is the reason for FD laws and increased attention on violations of insider trading rules. This is a rule you want to play absolutely straight, as the implications for both personal and corporate liability can be devastating.

You will need to have discussions with your management team and board about who can talk about what and when. I use these simple rules for everyone, and the penalties for violating them can be quick and severe:

- If the information has not been announced in a press release or discussed on a shareholder earnings call, it is not to be discussed with anyone outside the company.
- All board members should refer any calls to the company, as they are not authorized to speak on behalf of the company.
- Only the CEO, CFO, head of investor relations, and PR director are authorized to speak to investors and the public.
- Whenever there is a press or speaking event, at least one other person from the company must be present to take notes on what was discussed by the speaker.
- At the end of any press event or other speaking event, this scribe must call in-house legal to describe the topics addressed to ensure no additional 8K filing is required. (If you fumble and say something you should not have said, you do have a few days to make it public through an 8K filing.)

Of course, during the ramp-up to the IPO there will be customer presentations, symposiums, and such at which many different company employees will speak. All good, just make sure your in-house legal team vets any presentation before it is delivered. To do otherwise can open the door to all kinds of trouble, including a suspension of the IPO.

In this arena, the problem I see most often is a company's country general manager assuming it is okay to discuss local, country, or regional results; new customers; or employee headcount without regard to the impact of that information outside their purview. Here in the twenty-first century, news travels globally and fast. Just knowing that the Southeast Asia region did X amount in revenue can give analysts useful information that you (and the SEC) do not want disclosed.

So have a worldwide process in place for vetting all press releases (yes, even those in Southeast Asia) to ensure you are not unwittingly disclosing inside information.

With all of this done, the board should be ready to go to IPO.

CHAPTER 10

THE ROAD SHOW

About two months before IPO day, you start developing how you will describe both your business and your business model.

You should be pretty close to completion on the business section of your S-1. Using this as your guide, start building a thirty-minute-maximum pitch or road show deck. Keep in mind you have three tasks with this deck:

1. You want to tell a story about how the idea of your company or the need for your product line came about and why your customers are better off with your solution.
2. You need to tell a story about your business model and how it will evolve over time, up to five or even ten years from now.
3. You need to tell a story about your management team, what they each bring to the company, and how they will contribute to the execution and growth of the company.

STORYTELLING

In each of these categories, I tell a story with a plotline. By story, I don't mean a slog of PowerPoint slides you read with a drone in your voice. In fact, I intentionally limit the use of PowerPoint and rely on it only for meaningful images I want the audience to remember.

The conventional wisdom is to run through the pitch deck, then answer questions. But frankly, the pitch rarely does your business justice, and it's rarely memorable. Meanwhile, the formal Q&A, which is supposed to add to the audience's understanding of the business, too often ends up simply reiterating your boring slides.

I suggest a different approach. It is well known that storytelling is more effective than PowerPoint presentations. Even the best speaking coaches will tell you to start with a story in order to relate to your audience and get them interested in what you are about to say. Better yet, make it a personal story so the audience gets to know you.

I am convinced that if you can find two people in particular to assist in getting you ready for describing and selling your company stock, those two people should be a speaking coach and a writer to help you construct the story.

Neither form of help will come from your bankers, although they may have recommendations for speaking coaches. Rather, I suggest you look to the best presenters from TED talks, or university professors who are experienced at getting information to audiences when the audience may not know why they should be interested. Meanwhile, find a playwright or book author to help you tell your story.

At this point, you may be thinking, "Wow, that could be expensive!" You are right. But even if it costs $100,000, it will be cheap if the results help you sell $100 million-plus in stock and raise the value of your company to more than $1 billion. So find the best talent you feel comfortable with, and work with them. Also know that this is not a one-and-done exercise. Your business will evolve. Over the next few years you will have numerous opportunities to tell and retell the story of your business. Learn how to do this, perfect it, and find and nurture relationships with those speech and story experts who can help you.

The benefits of this investment will be enduring. Your management team will get better at painting a narrative vision of your company to your employees, your customers, and your investors. The payoffs in understanding and loyalty will be enormous.

The best thing about the JOBS Act is that it has established the concept of the emerging growth company and the recognition that sometimes a company's story needs to be tested and refined. There is a reason off-Broadway runs and previews exist for live theater: to polish the words and images created onstage. If you have ever seen the musical *Hamilton*, you know it is stunning in words, music, dance, and plot. But few people realize it took nearly ten years to polish and perfect the show before it was judged ready for Broadway.

No doubt, the plot was in place pretty early in the process. But the nuances of lighting, blocking, dialog, and music took up most of that decade. Obviously, you don't have that much time to perfect your story, but you need to take the same path. It helps to have good presenters, but in my experience most founders, with a little practice, can tell the story well because they lived it.

The two best founders I worked with were Marc Benioff and Howard Lerman. Both were masters of storytelling. But they also were committed to practicing and refining the presentation of those stories. Getting the rest of the management team—especially the CFO—to that level should be your goal. Now, admittedly, the skills these two have at storytelling and improvisation are beyond the reach of most of us. But with practice we can approach their level.

At our annual customer event at Yext, Howard involves the audience by pushing the envelope both with his story and the presentation. Most software demos—even if they are new and filled with great ideas—are rather boring. But at Yext we incorporate live theater and customer participation to demonstrate new ideas and solutions. At Salesforce, cofounders Marc Benioff and Parker Harris make a wonderful tag team as they incorporate humor and live customer participation as well.

At the end of the day, no matter the format, the key is to tell an engaging story, underscored by memorable images. Together, they are a powerful way to educate someone about your business.

TESTING THE WATERS

The "testing the waters" road show was valuable to Yext because it enabled us to experiment with different approaches to describing our business and to gauge how the audience received the story. We met with a select set of investors in various cities to see how our story was understood. Our tour, which took place one month before the IPO, started in New York City, where we quickly realized that we were not getting our message across. Later, on the train from New York to Boston, after a long day of investor meetings, Howard changed the wording and refined the message. As a result, in Boston we enabled our prospective investors to gain a significantly better understanding of our business.

For my part, I flew to Boston because I think trains take too long. Thankfully, Howard didn't go with me, because those three hours on the train gave him time to revise the message. The point is, set aside the time you need to refine your message after every presentation.

After we completed the "testing the waters" tour, we sat down once more to further improve and refine our message, even though the Boston presentation had been very successful. We drilled down on the nuances of the wording, the timing and effectiveness of examples, and the order of topics. Then we added one more polish of everything.

TIMING IS EVERYTHING

Several things happened back at the office while we were on the "testing the waters" road show. The finance and legal teams filed the confidential registration, and subsequently answered questions, clarified statements, and provided further commentary in response to the SEC's requests.

The good news is the SEC has a pretty good track record in terms of responsiveness, so once you have filed your S-1 in accordance with your planned IPO date, pretty much within a day you can learn when you can go public. That day will mark the end of your IPO process, but also the beginning of your relationship with thousands of new investors and shareholders.

In this two-month window before the IPO, many discussions will take place with the SEC on various topics. They will review your filing and ask questions around your disclosures regarding your business and the terminology used in your document and why you chose not to disclose what they consider critical information. This is a time where you work closely with your advisors to help sort out the proper response to satisfy the SEC examiners. These responses are critical, as they will live with you forever in the document you file every quarter with the SEC.

You will also be talking regularly with your chosen exchange. One of the tasks here will be to get on the exchange's schedule to ring the opening bell. Timing is everything, so close contact and continued relationship-building with the exchange will help get this set up. Once you do, you will want to move your road show schedule around to ensure you are at the exchange that morning.

What's the big deal about ringing the opening bell? Simply this: IPO day is one of the biggest lead generation days you will ever have, so you want to take full advantage of the publicity it generates. It is also the end of one process and the dawn of another. Formally marking a finish and new beginning is critical for the long-term success of the business. You need to get your employees focused on this new era, not on that day's stock price.

ON THE ROAD

Scheduling and planning the road show is up to you, so you need to decide where the trip will go and how long it will last. Be cognizant of the types of investors you are meeting. Make sure they own your benchmark company's stock. Also know who has held those shares the longest and who flips them.

The bankers have learned from experience that seven to ten days traveling the major financial centers in the U.S. is usually enough to get orders to sell your issuance. However, the road show is one of the few events during which you get to meet your future major shareholders and to make personal introductions with your key company executives. So instead of seven to ten days, consider two to three weeks, with the majority of your time in New York and Boston, but also a day each in Baltimore, Chicago, Los Angeles, and San Francisco. Then spend a few days in Toronto and London, one or two major cities in Western Europe.

Despite the pressure to get home, don't rush. Take the time to get the most out of the experience.

At Yext we did New York, Toronto, and London in one week. London was an exhausting twenty-four-hour side trip, but the London and Toronto meetings allowed us to meet some great investors. These days, the current incarnation of the standard IPO road show has eliminated these cities. We, in fact, were well received simply because we viewed these markets as important and took the time to travel there. The investor groups from those cities have been great to us ever since.

The Salesforce road show proved just as beneficial, but in this case it was with investors in Milan, Geneva, and London.

It is your stock to sell, but as you do so I want to remind you that your bankers will cater to their best customers. While you may not want hedge funds and short-sellers, your bankers will make sure those folks get an allocation. In other words, the process is rigged to some degree. So make sure you get to designate the big allocations to the investors you want and, whenever possible, avoid the folks you don't want.

A confession: there have been a number of investors I have met on my road shows that, while they may have been nice people, I really had no chemistry with. Because the supply of available shares was short, I chose investors with whom I thought I could build a strong relationship over time. You may want to consider doing the same.

Subsequent to the IPO, we have worked hard building and growing relationships with those key investors. Remember: people invest in you and your company to make money. If you do not deliver on your promises, all future investor meetings will be difficult, so you need to do your utmost to deliver expected results. But if you get into trouble, the goodwill you have developed with those investors will soften the blow and increase their patience.

Road shows are always intense. You are overscheduled, and you are utterly dependent on logistics and transportation, so private jets and car services are a must. You cannot do a road show on commercial airlines and with ridesharing—scheduling delays will kill you. Time is precious, so guard it.

Also, be adaptive and creative. On the Salesforce road show, once we got to Boston, we were stalled by a faulty part in the charter plane that was going to take days to fix. So we jumped over to Logan Airport to catch a commercial flight. As a result, we got in at 3:00 a.m., planning to start at 7:30 a.m. the next day.

This was a mistake. I forgot the first rule: it is your road show. There was no reason to start at 7:30 a.m. unless we wanted to. So I switched to an 8:30 a.m. start time. The attendees at the first meeting dealt with the delay, likely enjoying the extra time.

Remember: the banker support team is there to help and to make sure the logistics work, so take advantage of it. On all three road shows in my career I made sure that the support crew knew that I needed a Starbucks grande mocha, no whip, to start my day, and every morning one was waiting for me as I walked into my first meeting. Each of the folks I traveled with did something similar. Only Howard, on the Yext road show, got his own espresso. But I suspect he just wanted to go out and walk to mentally prepare for the day.

My point is this: you and your team will be running a marathon. As you embark on the road show, it's important to know in advance what you and your team will need to sustain sprint mode. Don't be shy about making those needs known to your support team.

By the time of the Yext IPO road show, Howard, Jim Steele, and I were older and wiser. We knew enough to try to make the tour fun. We took photographs and videos and sent them to our workmates. We ordered food we normally didn't eat at home. In my case, I even scheduled in some intervals for rest.

Even on the Salesforce road show, we did try to break the routine. For example, when we found out no one had ordered lunch on the plane for our flight from Milan to London, like an NFL quarterback, we called an audible. Much to the stress of the banking support team, we spontaneously stopped at a café and ordered a huge amount of Italian food for the flight. It turned out to be the best meal we had the whole trip, and the most fun.

A couple of guys I've traveled with over the years have even managed to get in some shopping time during road shows. Of course, that left me doing the investor meetings. But the mileage I got out of giving them a hard time made the sacrifice worth it.

One more note about your road show: make sure you have a photographer and videographer full time from the start of the road show to the end of the bell ringing, documenting your path. More on this later.

The typical road show ends in New York so you can be on the exchange floor for the company's first day of trading. But before that, there is one last task to do: price your stock.

PRICING NIGHT

Here's how stock pricing works.

It happens in the evening, most likely from 5:00 to 7:00, or later depending upon where the interest in your IPO stands. True to form, the underwriters will bring out all kinds of statistics, the most famous one being how many times the book (the available shares) is oversold. This metric is of interest, and a confidence booster, but not particularly meaningful, as there will be so many duplicate orders and so much jockeying by investors to get their desired allocation.

What is more important is the number of shares that would be purchased at various price points. Say you are offering ten million shares to the market. Generally, these should be primary shares—that is, shares the company is issuing and not secondary shares, those being sold by investors and employees.

In my career, of the three IPOs, only Pandora included these secondary shares. The problem with including this class of shares is that they are freighted with too much self-interest by the sellers, and often this results in the company taking a second seat in its own stock offering.

When pricing your primary shares, of course you want to get a proper valuation and price. But the best strategy is to provide for a win-win-win in the pricing. By that I mean it's not only the company that needs to get a fair price for the shares, but also the investors buying at the IPO who should get a fair price with some upside, and those who invested pre-IPO should get a good valuation too, one that can only go higher. Said another way, you want to price your stock so even in bad times the stock price won't go below the issue price. This sets a great goal for management to understand and respect the shares they are selling to other people who believe in the company, while allowing everyone to make some money.

Remember, it is not pricing day that establishes the valuation of the company, it is what you do every day after that impacts the valuation. To reinforce that philosophy, no one should be able to sell shares for the next six months (this is your IPO lockup). A reasonable valuation at the start sets everyone up to win.

When you have secondary shares in the initial offering, then the interests of the secondary shareholders come into play, and their sole desire is to maximize the selling price of the shares they have to offer. This played out at Pandora with those who had secondary shares. We were forced at the offering to meet their needs, and not the real market. The reverse was the case for Yext, where we might have gotten an additional dollar from the offering price, but we settled on $11 to ensure the transaction worked for everyone.

Keep in mind, though, that going public day is only a single point in time. In the long run, ongoing success is infinitely more important than that one day's price. Investors should see that your management has the confidence to play the long game. While employees and early stage investors deserve some near-term liquidity, it should not happen on IPO day.

A MATTER OF CONTROL

That brings me to one other point. Earlier I mentioned how sad it was that so many founders end up with just 10 percent of the company they founded after they raise funds and cash out. Well, often that happens because they cop out, sell their shares in advance of the IPO, and then set up a dual-voting structure. The dual-voting structure allows founders to control the voting shares of the company while shareholders have limited or no vote in the company's critical decisions. Such decisions include voting on different directors, voting to remove a CEO, and voting to merge or sell the company. Traditionally these decisions are made through one share, one vote.

When founders take control of the voting shares, it becomes a problem for the long-term health of the company, despite the argument that the founders know best in the long term. I submit when they took their money off the table by selling shares to other investors, they also lost the right to control the long-term outcome of the company. Those who have invested in the company should be able to make, through voting, the decisions affecting the company.

In my book, performance counts, and if the founders cannot perform, or raise the value of the investment over time, or if they take the company in a direction that is not in the customer's best interest, they should not be able to protect themselves with a special voting deal. In essence, in doing so they take their money early, but still get to control the company over the new holders whose money is now in the company.

Just as they did founding the company, the founders should continue to bet on themselves and the company at the IPO and afterward. Why should they not trust investors to do the same? Some argue that dual-voting tracks to protect the company from being taken over. But if the company is performing and increasing value to the shareholders, the odds of such investor behavior are pretty remote. In addition, there are well-known protections one can and should put in place to prevent a takeover. Creating dual-voting shares only signals that the founders bet on themselves until they sold out to a VC, and now they want their public investors to be stuck with them if something goes awry.

Sorry, that's not a fair trade.

ON THE EVE OF GOING PUBLIC

The pricing process ends on the eve of going public day. By now you've gotten the pricing committee to agree upon a price with the bankers. You have told your lead how you want shares allocated. The legal folks have gotten the paperwork signed and filed. A press release has been drafted. The market doesn't open until 9:30 a.m., so now you can open a bottle and toast to your team and yourself. (A bottle of Cakebread

Chardonnay is a great choice.) Then go home and get some rest; you've earned it, and you will need it. Tomorrow will be one of the biggest— and most fun—days of your business life.

CHAPTER 11

IPO DAY

I always look upon going public day as a single point in time. The hard work, the drama of getting to this day, the weeks with bankers going over details momentous and minor, the strain on the company management team, the herculean effort by the legal and finance teams, and the relentless, head-down work of days and weeks and months—it's now all behind us. This is a time to celebrate, to reflect, to enjoy, and to ignore the future for just one day.

My advice? For starters, wear comfortable shoes, as you will be on your feet all day. Have an enjoyable breakfast before the events begin. And most of all, enjoy the ride. There's nothing quite like it.

GOING TO MARKET

Waking up on going public day is always a bizarre experience. On the one hand, you are still exhausted from climbing the steep slope of the last few weeks. On the other hand, you are so excited you are nearly jumping out of your skin.

On IPO day, my wife and I always stay at the Mandarin Oriental Hotel on Columbus Circle in New York City. It's uptown, with Central Park across the street and a view of the Hudson River in the other direction. While sitting in my room, drinking coffee early on those mornings, it's pretty cool to realize I am ending one adventure and starting another.

I always take a moment to thank my wife for her patience and consideration during the years without breaks or holidays. We both plan to enjoy the day and splurge just a bit. After all, this is why I joined a start-up and stuck with it.

After breakfast we get dressed. This is one of those rare occasions when I put on a suit, but no tie. The NYSE is more casual these days. Then we are out the door—ready for a very special day.

The Salesforce going public day was especially exciting, not least because it was my first IPO. We had the full IPO road show team and key members of the company staying at the Mandarin Oriental—including the founders—along with their families. It looked like some foreign dignitary was staying at the hotel, given the long line of black SUVs and drivers outside on the street waiting to take us to the exchange.

Now, my wife is always thinking of ways to surprise me and make me feel special. That morning, as we were riding down in the elevator, she let me in on her secret: "We have special transportation taking us to the NYSE," she said, "so don't get in one of the company cars." I was intrigued.

As we walked out of the lobby, I could see the line of SUVs, but nothing more. Was our driver late? If so, we really needed to climb into one of the company cars. But my wife didn't blink. Instead, she walked along the queue of black cars, and I followed.

She finally stopped, turned back to me, and began to apologize. "I'm sorry," she said, "I guess I didn't get the right car service." There before me was our limousine: a dirt-brown, unrestored 1998 Buick.

My wife started to giggle, and I soon joined in. I yelled to my workmates that we'd meet them at the NYSE, and we piled into our old brown Buick. It was a wonderful reminder that even on this day of days, we needed to stay humble and grounded. I more than appreciated the thought, and when we finally got to the NYSE, we were still laughing. While I am sure I will forget many of the events of that day,

I will never forget my ride to the exchange and back to the hotel that evening.

In fact, the Buick became a ritual. To this day, we have tried to get that car and driver for each IPO. Indeed, whenever we get a car in New York City we are reminded of "our" car. I suspect that by the next IPO that old rust bucket will be scrap and the driver retired, but we'll find a comparable replacement.

Needless to say, my wife is unique—only she would make a twenty-year-old Buick a special part of a great day.

The ride from the Mandarin to the NYSE is about thirty minutes at that time of the morning. Yes, you want to get there early, and the NYSE has breakfast and special events lined up as well, so a 7:30 a.m. departure from midtown is usually about right. You run through Times Square, head down the West Side Highway, get off at some point, pass Trinity Church, and then turn around the corner to the NYSE entrance.

On that ride you think about your plans for the day, realize who you forgot to invite, and review the events that will be taking place back at the home office.

Let's talk about those events next.

PLANNING GOING PUBLIC DAY

IPO day isn't celebrated only in Manhattan. You can't take the whole company with you to New York, but you can bring some of that experience to the office. In each of my companies we set up televisions in our offices and served breakfast and champagne to celebrate the IPO and the bell ringing. The three-hour time difference means that the party usually begins at 6:00 a.m. in California.

Each company took a different approach to inviting the participants to the exchange and to planning the parties at the home office. Of course, the IPO is not the end game for a company, but only a new beginning. Still, you need to bring closure to your start-up phase and kick off the next great adventure: being a public corporation.

The early years of a company are like a strange race in which no one watches the start but everyone crowds around the finish line. Even there, nobody knows whether to cheer the achievement and big payoff or to mourn the loss of the company's simpler times and the rise of its new bureaucracy.

Well, I've never subscribed to that kind of pessimism, nor do I ever treat going public day as just another day. For me, it is the greatest day in the company's story—the end of an exciting past and the beginning of an even more glorious future. You can go back to work tomorrow; going public day is time for fun.

At Salesforce and Yext we had founders, early employees, executives, key employees, and spouses attend the NYSE ceremony and breakfast, introductions to key members of the NYSE, and meetings with the outside advisors. We thoroughly enjoyed the day.

The NYSE boardroom can hold a few hundred people, but you only can take a hundred or so people to the exchange floor. This can be tricky, so you may want to keep your crowd down to a hundred from the start. Personally, I recommend you take full advantage of this offer by the exchange management, even if it means leaving half the group behind in the boardroom. After all, most people never get to visit the mighty New York Stock Exchange, let alone the trading floor.

Pandora, by comparison, took a more conservative route. Founders, management, and board members held a nice party at the Oakland office, but keeping in mind that the party was at 6:00 a.m., it limited the participation.

In all three cases, I made sure the critical members of the finance team got to be in New York. After all, they had joined the company to help get the company public, so for them it would be particularly disappointing if they didn't get to see the big day in person.

Of course, we couldn't invite every person in the company who made this day happen. So we found a compromise. For Pandora's finance leadership, I flew them to New York and put them up in a hotel in midtown. Since they could not all go to the NYSE, we sent them to the offices of the lead banker to watch the process of matching the very first trade before it went live on the exchange.

We did this at Yext as well, though we invited a slightly larger group because Yext is a New York–based technology company, so the logistics were easier. The bank did a great job of providing champagne and pastries and getting the visitors as close to the trading station as they could, so they could hear and see the back-and-forth it takes to match, buy, and sell orders before trading begins.

In a way, this group visiting the bank trading floor is actually at the heart of the action, while the rest of us are just milling around the exchange trading floor, waiting for the bell ringing to open the day.

No matter what you do to celebrate going public day, here's the bottom line: be generous. Bring as many folks as you can to the opening bell, and for the rest provide some other memorable form of participation. Not only is it the right thing to do, but it will do wonders for morale both at the company and with the outside firms with whom you might want to work again.

ENTERING THE EXCHANGE

Now, I can't speak to the experience of arriving at NASDAQ on going public day, but I can describe to you the experience that awaits you at the NYSE. Before you enter, outside the building, you will see a huge banner showing your listing and ticker symbol. It is a great backdrop for a photo, and a great way to start the day.

Once you pass through the entrance, clear security, and pass through the metal detectors, you will be met by escorts to take you up to the NYSE boardroom. The elevators are new, but in a traditional style, and they take you somewhere, but it is difficult to know exactly where in the building you are. As many times as I have been to the NYSE, I still couldn't tell you where the boardroom is located.

Like everything, change occurs at the NYSE. Renovations had taken place a few times between my various IPOs. Though the experience is similar each time, the memories of the very first visit remain strong.

The first event with Salesforce happened before one such renovation, so I experienced some of the older history of the building. For example, as you came off the elevators, there was a barbershop, complete with old-fashioned barbers and warm, wet towels to clean you up after your haircut and shave. The other item of note (which my wife did not hesitate to point out): there was no women's restroom on that floor. Women had to go to another floor to find their lavatory. Needless to say, between the brown Buick and the lack of women's facilities, my wife and I will always remember our first visit to the NYSE.

Today, social norms have driven some changes: women will now find a restroom on the boardroom floor, but alas, the barbershop is gone. The boardroom, however, remains a classic, and though it too has been modernized, its history shows through. Having seen this room through its transformations has been an honor, just as I have seen the transformations of exchange CEOs from Dick Grasso to Duncan Niederauer to Stacey Cunningham. To my mind, despite the changes, the NYSE remains a sacred place.

Entering the boardroom on going public day reveals an unforgettable scene: your fellow workers gathered for the impending event in a place they probably have never been before. First-timers (and most of them usually are) are typically dazzled by their surroundings. They're introducing family members to coworkers, enjoying a grand buffet, while the NYSE folks describe the various historical events that have occurred in the room.

Oh, and here I must mention one of my favorite details: the NYSE visitor name tags. Everyone receives one. Those folks going to the exchange floor are given one type of ID tag; those going to the podium another. Why do I like them so much? They're not stickers with handwritten names, but real, metal name tags that bear the date and the event. I've kept every one of them.

THE EXCHANGE FLOOR AND PODIUM

Nine a.m. Eastern Time comes quickly. As the moment approaches, the exchange president goes to the speaker's podium in the boardroom to provide some color about the history of the exchange, the boardroom, and what is about to take place. For Yext, Thomas Farley, the president of the NYSE at the time, performed the honors.

Next is the presentation of the official company listing certificate and the handing of the medallion to the company CEO. On it is etched the name and date of the listing and if it is an opening or closing bell.

Then it is time to make your way to the trading floor and its famous podium.

Initial listings typically ring the opening bell. Listing on the NYSE has an added bonus: you can, and should, take advantage of anniversaries and ring the closing bell on the first anniversary of your IPO, and then every three to five years thereafter. It helps remind you why you are listed; it's a nice experience for new employees, and, honestly, it's just plain fun.

For Yext's second listing anniversary, we took the whole finance and legal team to the NYSE for the closing bell. It gave all fifty employees, many of them new hires, a chance to gather in the vaunted boardroom and then make their way to the trading floor. We did a lucky draw for ten members from this group to join me and three other finance and legal leaders on the trading floor podium for the closing bell.

Just fourteen people are allowed on the podium at one time, not just because it is small, but because the stairs are very narrow. When all fourteen people are up there it gets very crowded.

A side note: if you get the chance to do an opening or closing on the podium, make sure you look directly at the live feed video, and make sure you can be seen on the TV camera. It is not always easy; it can be so crowded up there that you can't shuffle. It helps to be among the first up the stairs. Don't be shy about being seen. I learned this from experience. You'll want that visual record.

Ringing the bell is rather simple, but it takes some thought and muscle. The button for the bell needs to be pushed, and with some effort. Your NYSE host will make sure you perform your task properly. For me, closing the market with the gavel, which comes right after the bell stops, with three sharp hammer strokes, is unbelievably cool.

AFTER THE OPENING BELL

Once you have rung the bell, and the NYSE has opened for trading on your going public day, you cheer and shake hands and then try not to trip and hurt yourself and others getting down those rather steep steps.

On the trading floor again, you make your way over to your market maker to wait for the opening trade in your company's stock. Often your founder or CEO will get some airtime on CNBC while waiting, as it starts broadcasting live from the floor of the NYSE exactly at 9:00

a.m. This gives your executive spokesperson a chance to explain what the company does, to thank folks for getting the company to this point, and to speak about the future. Sometimes the interviewer will prompt your spokesperson to address some of the challenges investors might be concerned about regarding the company.

The folks at CNBC are well informed and, honestly, at that hour both the trading floor and the network set are in complete chaos. It's a miracle that these media folks manage to look so cool on air. Having sat in the interview chair a few times, I can tell you that the experience is just crazy, and I am glad I survived. Luckily, the whole broadcast team does a great job of keeping you focused and at ease.

That said, there are occasions when things don't go so well, usually because the company spokesperson is so obviously nervous. That's why, no matter how good they think they are on camera, you must require media training for every person scheduled for live TV. Do not leave this to chance, because it is very likely that without that training, they will make a mess of it.

To further minimize the risk, on IPO day you should restrict the number of people who go on air to just one or two fully prepared individuals. Unlike the rest of the group, these designated interviewees should wear conservative business suits, and men should wear relatively plain ties. Keep everyone else in attendance away from the cameras. Also, despite the roar, everyone needs to stay silent, or risk getting picked up by directional microphones.

With this potential risk, why even do TV? Because the ROI is huge. Look up Pandora's IPO appearance on YouTube: it is almost seventeen minutes of uninterrupted airtime at the opening of trading. That is the equivalent of a million dollars of free advertising and promotion.

Why did this happen? Remember, Pandora invited its founders, senior executives, and members of the board to the exchange, to the trading floor, and to watch the first trade. We agreed in advance that only the CEO would do an on-air interview.

Well, the CEO did the interview, and superbly. That should have been it, but CNBC suddenly realized there were Pandora board members on the floor as well, so its reporters went remote, looking for those board members to answer one simple question, "When will you be profitable, since your business model doesn't seem to allow you to make money?"

To be fair, to extemporize an answer to such a question in a thirty-second sound bite would be challenging for anyone, especially when the CEO was the only person who had been prepped with an answer. So five different company directors were forced to stumble their way through their answers. All things considered, they did pretty well. My job at first was to monitor the CEO's response, but when board members started to be interviewed my job quickly turned into herding everyone off the trading floor and bringing this part of the event to a close. It was messy, but seventeen minutes on national TV to our target audience was definitely an upside.

There is always a learning curve to this experience. Lesson one: reinforce with your people that only one person from the company is designated to go on air. Lesson two, which I failed to learn at the time: if you are not the designated person to speak, then you have only one reply to every question, "I am not the proper person to speak for the company. You should speak with the CEO or some other designated spokesperson."

Watch the clip; it will be a significant learning experience. For me, it remains cringeworthy.

VALUATION

You have rung the bell, you have made the most of your time on CNBC, and the stock is about to open. You watch your market maker's trading panel (the panel is where the market maker sees all price movements in your stock and why everyone gathers around waiting to see the first trade), and all of a sudden your ticker goes crazy. Trading begins: up, down, back up, back down. Just crazy. At that point, the market determines the valuation, and your day at the exchange is coming to an end, even though it is only about 11:30 a.m. or so.

Return to the boardroom of the NYSE, collect your things, and head back to the hotel or out to lunch—whatever provides you inner peace. Starting tomorrow, you will have a larger group of shareholders.

They will have spent their money on you to execute and deliver results. No excuses. You need to be ready for that.

Usually, I go back to the hotel, have lunch with my wife—something simple but enough to provide an energy boost for what is to come. I'll do a conference call back to the company and the finance team to thank everyone and encourage them to enjoy the rest of the day, because tomorrow we start anew, and we'll need to take it up a notch as a publicly traded company.

That evening—and this is one of the most enjoyable aspects of going public day—my wife and I will host, at Locanda Verde in Tribeca, a dinner for the invited finance team leaders and their plus-ones. We consistently use Locanda Verde because it has a cool private dining room, and the food fits all dietary requirements.

At this dinner, we gather the invitees, make introductions, share a toast to our accomplishment, and enjoy a great meal with a great group of people. Most importantly, we provide the plus-ones a chance to see and meet the people their spouses or partners have spent so much time with over the last two years.

I love these dinners—so much so that we even hold anniversaries there. Even more fun, some members of the Pandora team have joined me at Yext, so our next anniversary dinner with the expanded Yext-Pandora team will be especially memorable. The point of all this is to bring together a great group of people, have fun, and revisit stories around our shared success. We celebrate our high points—the IPO, the closing bell—and we share one another's experiences of the day. After all, it is the people and the stories that you remember best and that matter the most.

Still to come is an IPO event at the company, where all the employees can celebrate together. That should occur within seven to ten days of the IPO, and most certainly on a Thursday or Friday, because experience has taught me that most employees don't show up the day after.

Why this interval before the celebration? Remember that photographer and videographer I mentioned, who have been documenting your journey since the road show? They'll need a week to ten days to edit the footage they've been shooting. Be sure the end result includes some humor and shows the sheer chaos of going public day. That way the rest of the employees can share the whole experience and get an idea of how demanding the road show and going public day really were for the participants. Save those images and video—they go into the company archives. After all, going public only happens once.

Most of all, enjoy every minute of it. Soak it all in. Then get some rest. Life after the IPO has begun.

CHAPTER 12

THE JOURNEY BEGINS

Wow, what a day it was yesterday! Well, strap in and clear your head, because now the work begins.

Forecasting, setting expectations, then meeting or beating those expectations, endless discussions with newly minted investors, and oh, by the way, you still have a business to run.

Your number one focus now is to get ready for your first-ever earnings call, just eight weeks away. This call sets the tone and expectations for going forward. In fact, this is the most critical earnings call you have to inaugurate your new duties as a public company. You are going to be very thankful you put all of those systems into place over the last two years.

The primary task right now is to help set the company up for success. Remember those three-to-five-year forecasts you handed to the sell-side research folks a few months back? Well, those estimates start having real impact now. From this point on, you must meet—or better yet, beat—those numbers you somewhat casually provided all those months ago. The sell-side research crowd will use those numbers for at least your first year, and sometimes even beyond.

Once you are back from your IPO adventure, it is important to dig in and look at your business—the state of inbound orders and your expected revenue, earnings, and cash flow.

As I said, you have about eight weeks before your first earnings call, so make sure your management team and your employees are fully engaged in creating a successful initial public quarter. In other words, as difficult as it will be, keep the stock ticker off everyone's computer, and stay focused upon the three or four measures of success Wall Street is looking for from your business. Take care of that, and the stock price will take care of itself.

Keep in mind the only things in your control that really move the company's stock price are the operating result you produce and the guidance provided for the next quarter and the full year. The rest, from the business cycle to events around the world, are beyond your control. Play a great game and there's no reason to look at the scoreboard.

REMAINING FOCUSED

So what are the critical factors you must focus on after going public day?

1. Running the business
2. Forecasting current and future results
3. Managing your cash (generated from the business and from your IPO)
4. Hiring, hiring, and hiring
5. Educating new shareholders
6. Dealing with the SEC

Let's look closely at each.

1. Running the Business

This task may sound simple—after all, you have been at it for a while. But remember, you have moved from AA baseball to the big leagues. There are no excuses at this level and no second chances; now you get valued on how you manage the business, your customers, and your employees, as well as a number of other factors. These include everything from new legal requirements for your growing workforce to international expansion with different business practices and currencies in those countries.

How do you do this? Think of it this way: human beings now can make sailboats that sail themselves and airplanes that fly themselves. They do so by making those machines monitor their environment and self-correct in real time. You need to do the same with your company: keep pushing to make the machine that is your company both efficient and self-correcting.

That means you need to automate your operations and make them routine, as much as you can. Look to cut cycle times on every process, and at the same time reduce the error rates of those processes. Make sure everyone on the management team and in your workforce understands that every day, every decision has an impact on the business and the valuation of the company.

Without this philosophy your team will continue to operate as if the company is still private, as if a one-day delay on getting a deal closed or a one-day delay on a collection is acceptable. The fact is now *every day* counts, not just the last day of the month or the quarter. In fact, by the time you hit those days, it is too late to course-correct any misdirections.

When running the financial side of the company, the challenge lies not only in forecasting (more on that next) and managing, but in keeping your processes and systems up to date. It also means staying ahead of the business so that your sales team and everyone else in the company who must deal with new processes and systems can learn them before they use them.

Further, it means paying attention to management meetings and keeping them effective, while holding people accountable for results, each and every day. To this end, I make it a rule to implement, immediately, a much more detailed look at weekly bookings and spending. I recommend this because part of your role is to optimize the business. Days come fast, and month and quarter ends seem to come even faster. That's why, when you see a letdown or weakness in your operation, you must address it quickly, and with a long-term fix, not a patch. Needless to say, that is much easier said than done, particularly when you are adding people and growing at a blistering pace.

As the company grows to encompass multiple locations, your challenges multiply as well. While a business may be run most easily out of a single site, often that business needs to be proximate to where their customers are. This inevitably forces the company to set up shop in multiple places in multiple time zones.

When this occurs, communications become exponentially more difficult. Time zones aside, phone calls and video meetings become the norm. Management at all levels now needs to adapt to running the business with folks who may not be physically present. The simple start-up days of the tight company family are gone forever.

Meanwhile, all sorts of new problems arise, such as managing effective conference calls. For example, think of how many times you have used a conference as an opportunity to multitask, checking your e-mail and such. How engaged were you during that call? Now map that over an entire organization and a hundred conference calls per day.

To minimize that chronic focus problem, I visit our different offices around the world. This way I can meet directly with team members in local offices and have employees at headquarters call in to the meeting.

Conference calls present a second, more difficult challenge: problem-solving. Problem presentation on a video call is easy; problem resolution is always hard. Too often people put off action "until we are together" at some undetermined time in the future. Guess what? That future date never arrives, and the problem is never solved. This is one reason big companies become glacial in their decision-making. So you must push your coworkers to at least start solving the problem while still on the conference call.

Adding different time zones to the process doubly impacts problem-solving. My response to that challenge is to rotate time zones, to help those on the fringes have some meetings during their workday. That way everyone shares the burden, not just the time zone farthest from headquarters.

When I worked in Asia, it was never fun to end my long day, have dinner, then jump on a call to the U.S. at 10:00 p.m. local time, while everyone in the U.S. was just getting started. They were fresh, while all I wanted was a glass of wine and some sleep. The converse was also true: I would have to start my day at 5:00 a.m., before I even had coffee, so the folks in the U.S. could have one last go at sorting out some issue before their day ended.

So you need to accept the new reality that you are now a twenty-four seven business. Time is fixed, and human circadian rhythms are not easily overcome, so give everyone a break by rotating your start times. You are also a public company, not a start-up, so your task is no longer a final sprint to going public day, but an endurance run to becoming a great, lasting company. This is yet another reason you need to remain constantly aware of other employees' needs. New rules apply. Self-awareness, team building, and consideration for others are now far more important.

Jobs that require a lot of travel also require special consideration. I learned that from one of my fellow executives at Hewlett-Packard. Whenever he came back from a long-distance business trip, he always blocked out a personal day—not for a holiday but as a day for catching up and reflection. At the time I found his behavior frustrating. After all, didn't every workday count? Wasn't he just being self-indulgent? What I came to learn over the years is that he understood something about himself: the days after trips were always physically and psychologically bad, and bad days led to bad decisions. Being tired and on edge does not contribute to positive relationships with, or confidence in, your team. This executive did not want to unload on his team simply because he was tired or not prepared to take on the issue at hand.

These days, I make my travel schedule more flexible, and those who want meetings with me have to wait until I get myself together and ready to make effective decisions. That said, I also ask those looking for a decision from me to provide me with some details in advance. That way, they can spend the intervening time further considering the issue and possibly coming up with answers without me.

2. Forecasting Current and Future Results

Although forecasting is always important, after the IPO it becomes vital to know just how the business is performing and to set expectations for the future.

There is endless debate about guiding Wall Street. In the early days of Google, the management team was determined not to set *any* guidance and to leave it to Wall Street to sort things out. That sounded radical, even brave, but the fact is the company still gave indications of the direction of its key business attributes. That's one way to do it, but not necessarily the one I'd recommend.

A second trend is for companies to append to their commentaries a statement like, "We are looking at the long term and not worrying about this quarter." Well, we all know they are looking just as hard at this quarter as every other company; they just don't want the stock market to get scared by recent news.

I seriously doubt any analyst or investor out there is fooled by these noble claims. The simple truth is that no company can function if it doesn't constantly look out three years, five years, and ten years, but they also must exhibit laser focus on how the business is doing daily, weekly, monthly, and quarterly.

I prefer to control my own destiny with regard to street expectations. I mean, who is better positioned to know this information than someone with my job title? Further, why not share some of that knowledge with Wall Street to help it better understand the trajectory of our business? Even if the company's path looks like a roller coaster, it's better for your investors to know now than to be surprised and react with anger.

My recommendation is that you push your outside legal advisors to provide indications of your first quarter after IPO and these same estimates for the full fiscal year as well. In fact, why not set expectations for the post-IPO year while still on your road show? After all, this information is critical for investors. So push hard to provide this information, not just on your road show, but in other marketing events for investors.

Keep in mind the investors already have your previous quarterly information. They see the trends, so why not set up your first-quarter success by providing an indication of results? That said, don't miss those forecasted numbers, as it will take at least two years to overcome that miss and the resulting damage to your credibility.

My approach is to provide the upcoming quarterly guidance on revenue and non–GAAP EPS and these same estimates for the full fiscal year as well.

A few thoughts on this approach: First, keep in mind the more elements you provide in your guidance the more you will be held accountable—and the more ways the street can discover something negative. Also, hold the company accountable to the guidance you have provided—not the street consensus that emerges from that guidance. Don't get me wrong—you can't ignore that consensus; just don't let it dominate your own communications. Instead, be well versed in your numbers. Run plenty of metrics around not only revenue and non–GAAP EPS, but also other key business metrics, including operating cash flow, deferred revenue, growth in sales reps year over year, billings, number of new customers, customer count, revenue per unit, and so on.

If you are observant, over time you will get a sense of what your investors are looking at, and you should measure those metrics too, on an ongoing basis. Many will prove useful to running your business—after all, analysts and investors aren't dumb. That said, you may find that some of the metrics they use shouldn't apply at this stage of your company's life—something you should point out to them.

For example, in the SaaS business, sell-side research is focused on the long-term value of a customer (LTV) and customer acquisition cost (CAC). While those metrics are useful in other applications, in this business they will lead you in the wrong direction when it comes to near-term investments in sales and marketing. Certainly, as the company scales and reaches $2 billion in sales, those metrics might start to make sense. But in the early stages of a SaaS company's growth, these metrics can hurt your business because they give you misleading information about your forward investments.

This happened at Yext where, the year before I started, the board had management focus on CAC and getting the ratio in line with normal metrics. Well, that meant reducing sales rep hiring when the company should have been investing in the future and adding sales reps. Listening to the street, the company had reduced its hiring of sellers and was on the brink of watching its revenues fall. Luckily, we turned it around by ignoring the metric, but it still took time to recover.

Investors finally figured out their mistake, but not before damaging a number of young SaaS companies. The lesson: look at the metrics your investors use, but don't slavishly follow them off the cliff. Rather, teach them why they are making a mistake.

Timing also can kill you. Red Hat was one of the first SaaS businesses. It provided analysts with guidance on revenue, non–GAAP EPS, cash flow, and deferred revenue. The company was well run and had a great business model. But its stock price was regularly hurt by bad timing, sometimes by just a day.

This is not a rare case. Take, for example, cash flow. Your company may believe it is in a position to make a precise forecast, but if a check doesn't clear the ACH (automated clearing house) or your lockbox and instead gets posted the day *after* the quarter's end, you are going to miss your guidance. The street then, despite your explanations, can still go off about you missing a guided number, and your stock price will drop the next day.

The truth is that it is very difficult to guide and make more than two numbers at any given time. If you can make your revenue guidance and non–GAAP EPS, the rest is mostly timing, and it will take care of itself. So provide only two guided numbers and move on. Keep the rest of your numbers in your pocket, in case you need to use them.

This means you should refrain from giving indications of direction for the other metrics that the sell side wants. Why? When you have, say, a $100 million business, your metrics almost always will be volatile month-to-month and quarter-to-quarter, and they will bear no real indication of the direction of the business. The reason for this? The law of small numbers says not all data will move the same way or at the same time as a transaction is recorded.

The good news is this: when you get to $2 billion, you will have enough of an installed base that the volatility will normalize.

At this point you may be asking why report non–GAAP EPS? In my methodology, non–GAAP EPS simply excludes stock-based compensation. Nothing else. Why? Because I don't control stock-based compensation expenses. Yes, I do control the shares I issue, but the fact is that the second driver is the stock price, over which the company has no control. Given that critical external factor, I don't believe including stock-based compensation reflects the ongoing day-to-day business of the company, so I exclude it. I suggest you do the same if you can get senior management to agree.

It follows that my non-GAAP number is very simple and straight-forward. Sometimes the accounting theorists just get carried away, and the rules don't reflect the real operating results of the company. This is one of those cases.

Again, you must forecast and stay on top of the business results to course-correct if something is amiss. Do not skimp on your forecast team, or on the tools they need to do their job.

3. Managing Your Cash

A critical part of the forecasting process is knowing your cash forecast. One of the key valuation metrics, next to growing revenue, is becom-ing cash-flow positive, or at least breaking even. Granted, business has a different quarterly sequence, but getting to cash flow break-even on a full-year basis—and staying in this zone—has a positive impact on valuation.

I do two cash forecasts. The first is forecasting the statement of cash flows, both from operations and from cash used in capital expen-ditures. This is easier said than done, because you also need to forecast your balance sheet to get to your operating cash flow (OCF) number. This number is an accounting representation of the cash used or gen-erated by your business.

Investors focus on the OCF number, with good reason. It is an indicator of whether you will need to raise more funds and possibly dilute their interest in the company. Also, it demonstrates the strength of your business model and your efforts to achieve profitability. So get your balance-sheet forecast process nailed down and in detail suffi-cient to complete an OCF forecast. In fact, make this activity a per-manent part of your five-year forecasting process. After all, managing cash is critical.

Along with doing the balance sheet and OCF forecast, I ask the person in charge of our bank accounts and treasury activity to do what I call a checkbook cash forecast. While accounting and forecast-ing OCF is critical for driving the business, the checkbook forecast is critical for daily cash management and knowing when and how you will make payroll. This forecast is very simple: you look at your cash receipts and your accounts receivable collection cycle, as well as other sources. Equally important is your timing in payments: when you pay your bills, when payroll is paid, when lease expenses come due, and such.

This type of forecasting puts an emphasis upon when you make certain payments. It ensures that you are not falling behind on these payments. It also helps you focus on making payroll. In many start-ups, this is the first step in managing your cash and knowing what it takes to fund the business going forward. Over time, and done weekly, these two forecasts discipline the company, keeping it focused on where funds are spent.

4. Hiring, Hiring, and Hiring

Before the IPO, on the road show, you described the future growth plans for your company. You may have, for example, announced the company's plan to expand internationally, add new products or features, and create adjacent opportunities to increase your total addressable market. Now you need to face the reality of those claims.

As you plot your future growth opportunities, you must consider the resources and requirements you will need to bring these opportunities to market. These investments need to be reflected in your five-year plan and in your cash forecasts. It is one thing to have ideas, quite another to invest in the future for a pay-off on great innovation.

The biggest and often hardest strategy to get right is recruiting and hiring the people who will help you move forward. Do not under-invest in your recruiting efforts. Build resource models that look at the number of hires needed each month and then work backward—the hiring funnel—to the number of inbound candidates you will need to interview, the number of candidates that need follow-up interviews on site, and the number of candidates you will successfully hire at the end of the process.

You aren't done yet. You also need to understand where, geographically, folks are needed and what types of skills are needed, and most importantly, you need a profile of a successful person in your organization. Keep in mind that this profile will change over time, so don't keep hiring folks based on an outdated template. The people you want to run a public corporation will not be the same personality type as those who took you public. They need different education, more global experience, and different communication and leadership skills.

There are two big differences in the profile of candidates you should look for now. First, you're no longer looking for the comparatively independent start-up hero; now you want a team player who communicates readily with all parties, up and down the organization chart. Second, you need people willing to share information with others in the company.

Start-up folks are great at getting stuff done, but only in their specific areas, not across the company. As the company grows it becomes increasingly important that people work together to achieve cross-company goals, rather than optimize for their own area of expertise. Start-up heroes typically have a gift for getting things done in take-no-prisoners fashion, and you need that in the early days. But that kind of behavior can have a negative impact on a maturing company.

5. Educating New Shareholders

Take advantage of all the information you can glean from your listing exchange and other financial services to understand who your investors are and how they approach investing.

Never forget that investors are people, not just numbers, and building relationships with each of them is important. Tech conferences, investor days, and ongoing phone conversations are good places to start.

At Yext, we are always inviting investors to stop by and see our offices and meet some of our executives. We constantly invite investors to our company's customer events as well. Why? Meeting your customers and prospects provides investors with a sense of how the company is doing. Also, you already know your investors will contact your customers directly, so why not facilitate the conversation in a positive environment? If you focus the company on customer satisfaction, these types of interactions with investors will almost always reinforce your business execution.

That doesn't mean you won't experience some negative feedback. But you can turn that around and make it useful as well. At both Yext and Salesforce we used negative feedback not only to get back to the specific customer and take action to regain their goodwill, but also to look at our delivery, to make sure the problems were one-offs and not systemic.

You don't have to like every one of your customers, but you should be interested in hearing their thoughts, because you can be sure that your investors will listen.

Finally, you need constantly to assess how investors view your business, making sure you are responding to these perceptions in earnings calls and presentations. Of course, some ideas are simply stupid. Over time you will develop the judgment to know which ideas should be addressed and which should be ignored.

6. Dealing with the SEC

Lastly, you need to stay compliant with the SEC. Keep up to date on future accounting changes. Also, track the latest SEC reviews of your benchmark companies and search for insight into any new changes that might materially impact your business. I stay aware of comment letters the SEC has issued for comparative and similar-industry companies, and I assess the implications for my company. Further, I recommend you gather relevant information regarding the latest rulings, new regulations, precedents, comment letters, and such and summarize them in a brief memo to decision-makers. Keep them informed about the changing rules of the economy so they can plan ahead.

LOOKING BACK

Once you've gone public, every once in a while, make sure you look around and notice how far you and the company have come. When you started this journey, you were part of a still-young start-up. Much of your work was improvised and reactive. You probably marvel (and perhaps shudder) to look back at how little the company really knew about its market, its customers, even its own operations.

Months after the IPO and beyond, the company you will see—even though it bears the same name and many of the same employees—is completely different. Much has been systematized and rationalized through the implementation of new systems, processes, and rules. You've replaced one set of investors, venture capitalists, with an army of new investors, shareholders. You now exist in the public eye in a manner that you never imagined, and you deal with numbers that are orders of magnitude greater than you saw back then. Eventually a majority of your employees will know nothing about life at the company before the IPO. What an extraordinary, exhilarating, exhausting, and rewarding journey it has been.

The journey to becoming a public company is demanding: implementing reporting systems, the road show, quarterly earnings calls, updates on the business, compliance with SOX and SEC rules, a broader investor base, and on and on. That's one reason why so many otherwise eligible companies don't take it. Why suffer all that aggravation?

And yet, for every objection, as you've seen, I can make an even stronger argument *for* going public:

- It makes you a better business.
- It makes you think through your investments.
- It makes everyone in the company accountable for the company's success.
- It rewards you with an increasing valuation and all the perks that come from building a successful company.
- It gives you greater access to capital.
- It creates wealth for your employees and investors.
- It improves customer loyalty by enabling them to connect with a verifiably successful company with a strong future.
- Building a lasting company can become a high-water mark in founders' lives, in some cases becoming the one achievement for which they are most remembered.
- Most of all, it gives everyone the chance to take part in the creation of a great, enduring company that they can look back on with pride.

Should you have any further hesitation in your decision to go public, consider the following: giant, historic companies such as Levi Strauss and Hyatt Hotels have recently gone public. Why go public now, after, in the case of Levi's, a hundred and fifty years as a private company? They want to provide more liquidity for their investors and to enjoy greater access to capital.

Recently, high-profile unicorns have gone public as well, mostly to get access to capital but also to allow earlier investors to liquidate their holdings.

The point is, eventually almost all successful companies do go public. History and my own experiences suggest that the optimal window to do so is when a company has between $80 million and $150 million in annual revenues. Beyond obtaining greater access to capital, liquidity, and wealth creation, these companies also are searching for higher visibility in the market and among customers.

Going public *is* difficult, but no more so than trying to run a private company without sufficient capital or with inadequate reporting systems or while losing key employees because you can't sufficiently reward them for their contributions. Life in a private company, no matter how successful, is insular; it is working in secret. Being in a public company is, by practice and by law, working in the public eye, with your financial status exposed to the world. That may sound scary, but on the contrary I find it refreshing and liberating. Ultimately, going public is rewarding, sometimes beyond your wildest dreams.

If you do choose to go public, congratulations! You're embarking on one of the greatest adventures and working toward one of the highest accomplishments attainable in a business career. Remember to enjoy the journey, even when it gets crazy. I wish you the best of luck along the way.

ACKNOWLEDGMENTS

It takes a team to bring a vision to reality. That is true of this book, the companies I've had the privilege to work with, and of my entire career. I'd like to acknowledge the people who have contributed to my success.

First my family. Thank you to my parents for the love and my earliest business lessons. Jack and Dolores Cakebread were classic entrepreneurs. Along with my grandfather, they ran a successful automobile repair business in Oakland, California, while also starting and building another successful business in Napa Valley, Cakebread Cellars. As I stated in the book, whether you go public or not is a choice. But first you have to have a vision and execute on that vision to create and sustain a successful business.

To my wife, Jill Cakebread. Her love and passionate dedication to whatever she is working on have taught me that staying committed in spite of challenges can lead to great outcomes. She has supported my commitment to three startups as they grew into public companies. Jill tolerated the daily grind, the postponed holidays and solitary dinners. She is as much a part of the success of these companies as I am.

On the business side, I want to acknowledge the leaders who took a chance on me early in my career and who continue to inspire me.

I was one of the lucky ones: I started at Hewlett Packard in the 1970s and worked directly with both Bill Hewlett and Dave Packard. They and many of the folks at this great company provided the foundation for my business acumen, leadership skills, and global business knowledge. During this time HP grew from $200 million to more than $18 billion in revenue. It was quite an education, and I am thankful for HP's willingness to provide that education to a graduate right out of school.

Thanks to Bob Bishop, Gary Lauer, and others at Silicon Graphics (SGI), a high-flying technology company at the heart of high-performance computing and the early days of the Internet. I enjoyed the continued exposure to global business and to the challenge of running a successful company when your whole premise is to make your products obsolete by introducing new solutions faster than your competition.

Thanks also to Carol Bartz and Eric Herr of Autodesk, who gave me my first opportunity as a CFO. Without their coaching and experience with Wall Street, this book could not have been written. I got a great education there—in communications, business excellence, and in the challenges of changing a business model.

Special thanks to Marc Benioff of Salesforce, who took a chance on a CFO with no start-up experience and certainly no IPO experience. To be part of making his vision become a reality, changing an industry, and creating one of the most successful software companies of all time has been a once-in-a-lifetime experience.

I am forever grateful for having the opportunity to bring Pandora, a pioneering streaming media company, public.

Thanks to Howard Lerman, Andy Sheenan, and Mike Walrath at Yext for allowing me to join them in changing the world of search. They enabled me to contribute to another vision and another important change in the technology industry.

Finance folks are rarely risk-takers by nature. However, I found people willing to take on the challenge and join me in turning good companies into great ones. My special thanks to Mark Abrahams and Martha McDonald at Autodesk. To the team at Salesforce with special shout-outs to David Schellhase and Kathleen Early. To Chris Martin, Delida Costin and Tim Regan for staying at Pandora. Plus Dominic Paschel, Trang Watson, Jared Waterman, and Selwa Hussain, who first worked to make Pandora a success, then joined me at Yext. And to Darryl Bond, who joined Yext and took the risk on a business that few people understood.

Finally, I'd like to express my appreciation for the people I've worked with outside of these companies. Specifically, the presidents of the New York Stock Exchange—Richard Grasso, Duncan Niederauer, Thomas Farley, and Stacey Cunningham.

To the team at Silicon Valley Press, especially Joe DiNucci and Atiya Dwyer for their help with this book. And to Andrea Grindeland for taking on the challenge and helping get the word out.

Finally, again to my wife, Jill, and her daughters, Jennifer and Haley. Their support for my work and for this book has been invaluable.

Thank you all!

APPENDIX

GOING PUBLIC TIMELINE

ACTION	DEADLINE
INTERNAL CONTROLS	
Revenue and Booking Contract Approvals and Rules	24 months
Approval Matrix	24 months
Signing Authority	24 months
Finance—Retrospective Review of T&E	24 months
Resolve External Audit Management Letter Comments	18 months
Systems Change Management	12 months
Formally Document Process Description Controls	12 months
Internal Audit Function/Person	12 months
Disclosure Committee / SEC Reporting Certification Process	6 months
REVENUE RECOGNITION / SALES COMMISSIONS	
Daily Revenue Recognition System Changes	24 months
Daily Revenue Recognition Transaction Rules	24 months
Formal Bad Debt Policy	24 months
Amortized Sales Commission System	18 months
Amortized Sales Commissions Rules	18 months
Credit and Collections Team (Credit Checks, Aging Review, etc.)	12 months

SYSTEMS

Salesforce Data Definition Updated and Consistent	24 months
NetSuite Phase 1 Implemented but not Integrated	24 months
Coupa Phase 1 Implemented but not Integrated	24 months
Anaplan Implemented but not Integrated	24 months
Expensify Implemented but not Integrated	24 months
Zuora Implemented but not Integrated	24 months
Contract Management Tool	
(Integrated with Salesforce and DocuSign)	21 months
NetSuite Phase 2 Integrated	18 months
Coupa Phase 2 Integrated	18 months
Expensify Integrated	18 months
Anaplan Integrated	18 months
Zuora Integrated	18 months
Blackline Implemented	18 months
System Requirements for New Revenue Standard	12 months
Transfer Agent/Registrar	12 months
Xactly Integrated into NetSuite	12 months

BUDGET/PLAN/FORECAST/REPORTING

Monthly Account Reconciliations	24 months
Monthly Actual Reporting to Budget and Forecast	21 months
Monthly Expected Results Forecast, 24 Months Rolling	18 months
Monthly Barometer/KPIs (Build-up Over Time)	18 months
Monthly Financial Package (F/S and Account Analyses)	18 months
Build Out Financial Reporting (Headcount, XBRL, etc.)	12 months
Statutory Financial Reporting for International Subs	12 months

GAAP ACCOUNTING

Fixed Assets (Inventory, Write-off, Controls)	24 months
Complete Audits (FY)	24 months
Valuation/Acquisition Accounting	24 months
Revenue Recognition Agreed to with Accounting Firm	24 months
Stock Comp and Equity Base Validation	21 months

Monthly Process for Tracking and Updating Option Activity	21 months
Asset Tagging and Controls	18 months
Quarterly Reviews for Accounting Firm	18 months
Deferred Commission Accounting Agreed to with Accounting Firm	18 months
New Revenue Standard Agreed to with Accounting Firm	12 months

TAX/TREASURY/BUSINESS RISK

Business Insurance	24 months
D&O Insurance and Indemnification Agreements	24 months
Commercial Cash Setup, All Subsidiaries	24 months
State Sales Tax Resolutions	24 months
VAT/GST Implementations	24 months
Transfer Pricing—Intercompany Agreements	18 months
Legal Entity Tax Planning Proposal	18 months
Investment Policy and Compliance	12 months

GOVERNANCE

Informal D&O Questionnaire and Independence Review	18 months
Audit Committee Meetings Charter, etc.	18 months
Nominating and Governance Meetings Charter, etc.	18 months
Board Corporate Governance Guidelines and Practices	18 months
Retain Compensation Consultant for Directors and Officers Process	18 months
Executive Expense Reports Review Quarterly by AC	18 months
Formal D&O Questionnaire and Independence Review	6 months
IPO Update of Committee Charters	6 months

INTELLECTUAL PROPERTY

Trademarks (U.S.)	24 months
Foreign Trademark Filings	24 months
Domain Names	24 months
Patent and Patent Continuation for Existing Products	21 months

MARKETING & PR

Website/Product Claims Review	18 months
Crisis Management Plan	12 months
Factsheet with Support for Market and Product Statements	12 months

PUBLIC COMPANY COMPENSATION TRANSITION

New Equity/Cash Incentive Plan(s) to be Adopted at Listing	12 months
Employment Agreements with Executives	6 months

COMPLIANCE AND GENERAL

701/Blue Sky Compliance	24 months
IP/Trademark Policy	18 months
General Internal Due Diligence Review (TBC Through Year)	12 months
Data Protection and Marketing Practice (U.S.)	12 months
PII, Data Protection, and Marketing Practices (Int'l)	12 months
Code of Conduct Training	12 months
Antibribery/Trade Controls Risk Assessment and Policy	12 months
Records Retention Policy	12 months
Open Source Compliance Diligence and Review	12 months
SOC II Compliance Policies	12 months
Capital Structure Changes (if needed)	12 months
External Communications / Social Media Policy	12 months
Compliance Training	6 months
Whistleblower Hotline	6 months
Insider Trading Policy and Exec Officer and Restricted Employee Determination	6 months
Public Company External Communications and RegFD Policy	6 months
Public Company Charter and Bylaws to Be Adopted at Listing	6 months
Internal Draft Prospectus	6 months
Investor Relations Website	3 months
Other SEC/NYSE-Required Policies	3 months
IPO-Related Employee Trainings	3 months

INDEX

ABOUT THE AUTHOR

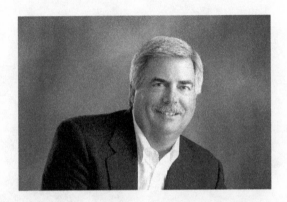

Steve Cakebread led the financial teams that took Yext, Pandora, and Salesforce to successful initial public offerings. He is a recognized expert in preparing for IPOs and is a regular speaker on the subject. Earlier in his career, Steve served as CFO for Autodesk, vice president of finance for Silicon Graphics, and director of finance for Hewlett-Packard. Steve earned his bachelor's degree in business from the University of California, Berkeley, and his MBA with a focus on international finance from the Kelley School of Business at Indiana University.

CPSIA information can be obtained
at www.ICGtesting.com
Printed in the USA
LVHW091214301020
670120LV00003B/4/J